W9-AMY-210

LIBERIA

Also by CHARLES MORROW WILSON

Empire in Green and Gold

Ambassadors in White

Middle America

Central America

Trees and Test Tubes

CHARLES MORROW WILSON

LIBERIA

WILLIAM SLOANE ASSOCIATES, INC.
Publishers *New York*

First Printing

PRINTED IN THE UNITED STATES OF AMERICA

Contents

LIBERIA

Chapter One

From the Eternal Jungle

THIS BOOK is a story of Liberia, the only republic in Africa and one of the two Negro republics in our present-day world. Haiti is the other.

During 1947 Liberia celebrated its hundredth anniversary as a republic. Appropriately and optimistically the theme of its celebration was "West Africa in a World of Peace." Its century-old motto, "The Love of Liberty Brought Us Here," remains intact.

The Republic of Liberia fronts the Atlantic from the underpart of the huge bulge of West Africa. It is in the deep tropics between latitudes four degrees and seven and a half degrees north. On the land side it is hemmed in by the British colony of Sierra Leone, French Guinea, and France's Ivory Coast Colony. Except in the dry season, from November to March or April, the climate is rainy and in view of the latitude fairly cool. The dry season is the hot season.

As the solitary republic in a continent of subject colonies, Liberia is a gateway into Africa of immense value to the democratic world and particularly to the United States.

History books usually recount how Liberia (the name is the Latin *liber* with *ia* added for euphony) originated as a "refuge" for freed slaves from the United States, and how the colonizing began in 1822 under the auspices of the American Colonization Society—with the helping hand of President James Monroe for whom Monrovia, the remarkable Liberian capital, was named. But most of the books fail to make clear the truth that fewer than 1500 American

Negroes actually braved the fever-ridden frontier called Liberia, or that fewer than half of one percent of present-day Liberians are descendants of American Negroes.

In a sense Liberia is American-born. But in a far more literal sense the country is of the real Africa, with its picture-book jungles, hammock trails, stick bridges, and cone-roofed huts built of mud and thatch. Even the freed slaves who in 1822 started the "Commonwealth of Liberia" (and suffered a fifty-percent casualty rate from malignant diseases while so doing) were West Africans only briefly removed by the slave trade. During July 1847 a handful of Negroes, most of them former Americans, proclaimed Liberia a republic and drafted a constitution generally like that of the United States except that suffrage and property ownership are limited to "persons of African descent." During the first sixty years of its life the United States did little to help the Negro republic, and Britain and France combined to gobble nearly half of the original land area. Nevertheless, Liberia has lived past its century mark.

Most of the country is rolling and heavily forested. Contrary to the reports of various of the early explorers, several of whom told of "mighty mountains towering 10,000 feet above the sea,"* Liberia is not mountainous. Though some of the interior is still unmapped, when you fly over the country in a plane you do not see any mountain peaks higher than perhaps 4,500 feet. In adjoining French territory there are landmark mountains such as those in the Druple Range (9,840 feet) and Great Nimbe (6,560 feet). but the average elevation in Liberia is well under 1,000 feet. All this makes for a land of rain forests.

From a plane window one sees that coastal Liberia is for

---

*Sir Harry Johnston, *Liberia,* Vol. 2, p. 482. London, 1906.

the most part low country spotted with outcroppings of black volcanic rock. The vegetation tells clearly that the rainfall is heavy, ranging from 90 to 170 inches a year, which is from two to six times the rainfall averages of the United States east of the Mississippi. Liberian rainfall varies tremendously—as much as 80 inches yearly—in specific areas only a few miles apart. But the jungle growths and the changing foliages also indicate that the country is not excessively hot, in the sense that coastal Central America and other seafronts warmed by the Gulf Stream are hot. Off the west coast of Africa there is a cool ocean current. One observes, too, that the many rivers of Liberia move tortuously into the Atlantic and frequently block the ocean front with large accumulations of sand and alluvial earth. The blockaded river mouths constitute a serious obstacle to river traffic.

Forests predominate inland except on occasional rock-littered mesas. If the plane stays within two thousand feet of the ground you will see scatterings of banana or plantain trees, dark green mounds of oil palms, and occasional grass lands. Here and there on low hilltops or in valleys are the native towns. In case you have a pocket compass, you will notice, even in a plane, that the needle of the compass leaps violently, for the earth is heavy with iron and the day may come when Liberia will be an important source of American iron.

Swinging eastward and down the coast the hills become fewer and lower, and the tall forests are only occasionally broken by splotches of cleared lands. Most of the tribal villages in this area are built on the narrow plateaus, and the rivers carry considerable traffic of dugouts and native canoes.

Swinging farther east below the great bulge of Africa you see the fingered promontory of Cape Palmas, where the fabled palm groves reported by early explorers no longer exist. Then you see the twisting Cavally River whose left bank is now the far inland boundary of Liberia. East of the muddy Cavally are the great wild-elephant pastures of French Africa. In these lands there is at least a chance that you may look down on a herd of elephants roaming about or rooting up trees and leaving swaths of forest ruins that look like the ravages of an Arkansas tornado.

Before the air age you entered Liberia by way of the port capital, Monrovia. Ship travelers still enter that way. Heading inland or upcountry from Monrovia by auto you follow a graded earth highway that parallels the low, sandy coastline for about ten miles; then turns northeast to pass through Mount Barclay plantation, the nation's first planting of Hevea rubber trees; then on to the thatch-roofed village of Careysburg; then toward the ancient crossroads of Kakata and the jungle of the interior. At present Liberia has about 400 miles of public roads, completed or in the building – which is probably no more than one-tenth of the minimum need. In the backcountry the brief spans of cleared roads end head-on in blockades of jungle, and most of the river crossings still lack bridges.

Africa is huge. In all it covers nearly twelve million square miles, which is about half again as big as North America and almost four times the area of the United States. Today there are at least 150 million Africans. Liberia is but a tiny dot on the continent, its land area being about 45,000 square miles, slightly bigger than Ohio. Though there has never been an official census, the population is estimated as 1,600,000, of whom well over 95 percent are members of indigenous tribes. The tribes remain a vital part of the nation, and the government of Monrovia takes accurate and sympathetic account of their needs and viewpoints. This situation makes Liberia particularly representative of Africa and African destinies.

Liberia has been a loyal ally of the United States in both World Wars; its part in the second was of particular benefit to the United States and the other United Nations. On December 3, 1942, the African republic became one of the United Nations and as an ally made available her lands, harbors, crops, people, and other resources for the use of the Allies.

This was more than a gesture. Liberian Hevea groves provided a substantial part of the rubber so essential to the fighting forces. Also, Liberia supplied several of the war's most important air bases, particularly the great land-plane and bomber base, Roberts Field, and the strategic seaplane base at Fisherman's Lake. Long-range bombers of the U. S. Army Air Forces and the Navy Air Command and of the Royal Air Force (as many as 17,000 per month) received shelter, bombs, fuel, miscellaneous supplies, and combat personnel at the great air bases of Liberia and from them proceeded to batter, harass, and paralyze Nazi supply lines and bases in North Africa and the Mediterranean, to help break the back of Rommel's Afrika Korps, and in time to spearhead the Mediterranean offensive.

All this has become history. But the fact that the United States through the U. S. Navy has recently completed at Monrovia, Liberia's ocean-front capital, one of the most strategic navy bases and deep-water harbors in the world bespeaks Liberia's importance to global planning.

Liberia is essentially and habitually a nation of peace; a republic which has never suffered a revolution or a major civil war; which has never impeached or violently deposed a president; which has never had a president or a national leader who was not lawfully elected to office. This book is principally concerned with Liberia as a nation at peace and with her contributions to a world at peace. It deals with Liberia as a nation in growth, as a laboratory of the tropics, and as a stronghold for the production of natural rubber.

Liberia is a fertile and typical part of a great continent which quite conceivably can be the garden-land of humanity.

Chapter Two

From North and West

THE REAL story of Liberia, which is not well known even in West Africa, is a few pages of America shuffled into a vast encyclopedia of Africa, but the American pages are indispensable. Liberia as a nation was born of an American ideal and an American philosophy.

The story goes back a long way in time. Three years before the American Revolution began, Samuel Hopkins published in Boston a plan for training freed Negroes of the United States as colonizers and missionaries for Africa. Eight years later, in 1781, Thomas Jefferson revived another plan for the gradual abolition of slavery in the United States by means of methodical deportation and subsidized colonization abroad of freed slaves.

At the beginning of the American Revolution the American colonies had a considerable population of freed Negroes, probably several hundred thousand. Some of the Negroes had been liberated by voluntary consent of their owners; others had been freed after their rescue from slave-trade ships by British or colonial police authorities; still others had run away from their owners and gained sanctuary in non-slave territory.

Long before 1776 a great many Americans had come to consider slavery immoral and wrong. By 1794 the Congress of the United States began enacting laws to end the slave trade between the United States and foreign powers. During 1800 and again in 1803, on recommendation of Thomas Jefferson, Congress enacted an almost complete prohibition of slave importation. Again in 1807, Jefferson's final administration succeeded in passing a more rigid statute.

But the "African" statutes were flagrantly and stubbornly violated. The slave trade continued and the population of freed Negroes grew. The problem of the "unkept Africans" became increasingly appalling to slave-owners generally, and to many non-slave-owners, and was the subject of some state legislation. As early as 1800 the Legislature of Virginia had requested the Virginian members of the Congress to "correspond with the President on the subject of purchasing land without the limits of this state whither persons obnoxious to the law or dangerous to the peace of society may be removed."* The request referred plainly to freed Negroes. It recommended Africa as an appropriate site for their resettlement, but failed to mention any particular part of Africa. The motive was a far cry from philanthropy or social endeavor. Owners of slaves feared the presence of freed slaves.

During 1818 slave-trading was formally defined as piracy by the Congress of the United States. A supplementary act, dated March 13, 1819, provided that Negroes captured from slavers should be "safely kept, supported and removed beyond the limits of the United States."* The President of the United States was authorized to make "proper negotiations" with residents of the coast of Africa as agents for receiving Negroes taken from captured slavers by vessels of the U. S. Navy and Coast Guard. The act of 1819 appropriated $100,000 to carry out the program described.

Meanwhile, beginning in 1817, the American Coloniza-

---

*Message from the President of the United States (W. H. Taft) to the Committee on Foreign Relations; March 25, 1910.

tion Society had appeared in Eastern seaboard cities. Instituted largely by missionary groups, the Society had been semiformally adopted by the state legislatures of Maryland and Virginia. Henry Clay supported the Society ably, as did John Randolph and other prominent political figures of the times. During March 1818, the American Colonization Society had dispatched a ship and a committee to negotiate for a colony site near Sierra Leone (immediately north and west of what is now Liberia), a West African territory which the British were in the process of taking over as a refuge for freed slaves of the Empire.

During these times "Liberia" was still known to traders as the "Pepper Coast" or "Grain Pepper Coast." The American colonization committee chose Sherbro Island, now a promontory of the Liberian coast, as a colony site, but realized somewhat belatedly that the Society had no money with which to purchase the land from the native chiefs.

However, in 1819, President James Monroe officially approved the purchase of the site chosen by the Colonization Society, and sent two representatives, the Reverend Samuel Bacon and John P. Bankson, to complete plans for a colony of American freed Negroes. The agents were instructed somewhat confusingly: "You are not to connect your agency with the views or plans of the American Colonization Society, with which under the law the Government of the United States has no concern."

In any case, the American Colonization Society and the Government of the United States proceeded as one. Reports of the Navy Department showed that Federal funds as appropriated were used to "colonize and build huts for recaptured slaves and to provide the latter with farming utensils, teachers, arms and ammunition." But the appropriation was so inadequate that Congress supplemented the initial $100,000 grant with several smaller appropriations averaging around $4,000 apiece.

Late in 1819 President Monroe's agent chartered the *Elizabeth,* a commercial sailing ship, to carry a group of expatriates back to Africa. On February 6th of the following year, the *Elizabeth* with 86 freed Negroes aboard and convoyed by the *Cyane,* a sloop-of-war of the United States Navy, sailed out of Philadelphia for West Africa. On arrival at Sherbro Island the voyagers learned that the Kru tribesmen of that coast steadfastly refused to sell the island site. As the ship waited at anchor pending negotiations, its passengers were racked with tropical fevers and dysentery. Twenty-nine of the eighty-six Negroes and both of the President's agents died. The survivors were put ashore at the British settlement near Freetown in Sierra Leone.

During 1821 the perilous venture was revived. This time James Monroe dispatched the brig *Nautilus* with twenty-eight freed Negroes aboard – every one of whom knew that his life was in maximum peril. The Navy brig carried the passengers and their supplies to a location near Cape Montserado on the Pepper Coast. Again the native tribesmen refused to sell their land, so the emigrants were shipped back to New York.

Meanwhile, the President of the United States, with shortening temper, appointed Dr. Eli Ayres as colonizing agent and dispatched the Navy's armed schooner *Alligator* as escort for a repeat performance.

Returned to Montserado, Lieutenant Robert Field Stockton, U.S.N., commanding the *Alligator,* went ashore and "energetically persuaded the natives" to sell to the American Colonization Society a strip of land 130 miles long and 40 miles deep, to be used perpetually for the settlement of

American freed slaves. There is no record of what the chiefs were paid for this coastal strip, which remains the home land of descendants of the American colonizers. Presumably the purchase was paid for with trading goods, such as muskets, calico, umbrellas, gunpowder, lead balls, and tobacco. That, at least, is indicated by the minutes of the American Colonization Society. The first settlement was raised fronting the sea, and named Monrovia in honor of James Monroe, fifth President of the United States. Both "Monrovia" and "Liberia" were names invented and suggested to the American Colonization Society by an American, one Robert Goodlowe Harper of Baltimore.

Beset with hunger and ravaged by fevers, the little colony writhed and wavered but somehow lived. During 1822 the State of Maryland and the Maryland chapter of the American Colonization Society raised still another fund, with which to build mud-and-thatch huts and to dispatch additional American Negroes to the jungle-edge refuge. This was the trip on which Jehudi Ashmun and his wife went as "spiritual shepherds."

Born in 1794 near Champlain, New York, son of an extremely poor white family, Jehudi Ashmun – destined to be known as Liberia's Prophet Jehudi – had worked his way through four years of Middlebury College in Vermont, then entered the Congregational ministry and became organizer and principal of a charity school at Hampden, Maine. In 1818, at the age of 24, Ashmun went to Baltimore to become editor of the *Theological Repertory,* then a feeble periodical of the Episcopal Church. There he began to support the cause of a colony in Africa for freed slaves – a cause that was soon to be justified.

For in 1821, only four years after the Colonization Society was founded and just as Prophet Jehudi was preparing to leave for Liberia, a serious slave revolt was taking shape in South Carolina. Its leader was a remarkable freed Negro named Denmark Vesey, who lived in Charleston and there worked as a freed tradesman. Late in 1821 Vesey began to select conspirators for an uprising of slaves. He chose mostly literate Negroes, among them Mingo Harth and Peter Poyas, but also one "Gallah," a big fighting man who professed to know nothing more than the language of fists, knives, and blood. Vesey was a scholar. He spoke French, Spanish, and German as well as English. He used the Bible to prove that God had ordained that all slaves be freed of bondage. In considerable part he organized the revolt by the forthright process of reading from the Scriptures.

With time and skill Vesey and his organizers mustered a following of between seven and nine thousand slaves, men and women, and shaped them into a well-disciplined band of conspirators. Discerningly, Vesey limited his followers to craftsmen and farm laborers, ruling out all household slaves as untrustworthy. By gradual stages he collected and cached 250 bayonets and pike heads and at least 300 daggers and swords, for the most part fashioned in plantation smithies by Negro blacksmiths. Several Negro barbers were commissioned to make wigs and false whiskers with which to disguise the better-known conspirators. In Charleston he detailed followers to spy out every store or house with arms and ammunition and assigned others to commandeer all horses from Charleston stables.

Late in April 1822, Vesey decided on the second Sunday in July as the date of revolution, which projected close-in attacks on the city of Charleston from five different areas.

Then an unnamed informer caused the arrest of Peter Poyas and Mingo Harth, Vesey's ablest lieutenants. When neither was convicted, Vesey resolved to set the date of the uprising ahead by a month. But before the time was ripe another slave turned informer. At that, all the leaders were arrested and thirty-seven of them, including Vesey, were hanged between June 18th and August 9th. The story of the planned revolt frightened slave-owners throughout the South and gave rise to violently repressive legislation: laws prohibiting the hiring out of slaves, laws demanding the appointment of a guardian for every freed Negro over fifteen years of age, laws to prohibit the education of Negroes, and more laws to prohibit the congregating of slaves.

But Jehudi Ashmun contended that slavery is not only morally but economically wrong. He predicted that its continuation would only throw all the United States into chaos and ruin and recommended that the U.S. Government purchase all slaves from citizen owners, pay for them outright, then resettle the freed people in Africa and there help them found a Republic of Negroes. Unlike many "abolitionists" Ashmun had the courage of his convictions.

So in 1822, at 28, Jehudi and his wife Mary set sail from Baltimore in charge of 37 freed Negroes who on order of President Monroe had been loaded on the brig *Strong* for resettlement in the African coastland called Liberia. Arrived in the newly founded "commonwealth," Ashmun promptly discovered that at least a third of the previous 114 settlers had died of fevers, and that most of the rest were sick. Of the two original "agents" one had died and the other had deserted the colony. There were grim rumors to the effect that certain native tribes were already undertaking to destroy finally the pitifully feeble colony. Ashmun could muster only 27 men who were strong enough to bear arms. Previously the U. S. Navy had provided two small brass cannon and a little gunpowder. Jehudi led the men in building breastworks and collected all available weapons.

Just as he finished the defense work at the jungle edge, his wife died of malaria. The prophet carried on. Presently the long-dreaded attack came. On November 11, 1822, shortly before dawn a force estimated at 900 savage tribesmen swept down upon the little colony. Ashmun wheeled out one of the tiny cannon, stood with a match in hand, and—as the jungle Negroes pushed near—lighted the charge of grapeshot. It mowed down at least twenty of the attackers. But the jungle Negroes rallied and charged again. Ashmun then directed the firing of both cannon. The tribesmen re-formed and charged again. Several of Ashmun's men had been killed by spears. But the prophet once more loaded a cannon and fired it into a "solid mass of human flesh." That stopped the attack. Returning to his own force, Jehudi counted four men dead and four severely wounded. The siege continued. Each night for the next three weeks the colonists mounted guard day and night. From the jungle came the constant beat of war drums. When the final attack came, Jehudi Ashmun once more fired the defending cannon. That ended the siege.

Then the frail warrior from upstate New York undertook to show his people how to clear land, build fences, plant gardens, and establish crops. In time he renewed his exhortation that all Negroes in the United States be freed and helped to honorable settlement in West Africa. But Jehudi Ashmun had no armor against jungle-edge diseases. His health became worse. In 1828 the remarkable prophet returned to the United States and died in New Haven only a few days after his arrival there, tired and old at 35.

During the six hard, hot years that followed, approximately two hundred additional freed Negroes arrived. At yearly intervals American Navy craft called to "view" the colony and to deliver supplies, desperately needed and usually inadequate. The hazards of disease, hunger, and embittered native tribesmen continued.

Nevertheless, other colonization societies, organized in and sponsored by individual states, began to found separate settlements on nearby coastal areas. The Maryland "department" of the Colonization Society undertook to establish a settlement at Cape Palmas, about 270 miles down the coast from Monrovia. That colony, specifically designated as "Maryland in Liberia," acquired its own constitution and bill-of-rights. Then colonization society groups of New York and Pennsylvania established a freed slave colony at Bassa Cove. A Mississippi society founded the jungle-edge community of Greenville. During 1837 all the settlements except "Maryland in Liberia" joined to form the Commonwealth of Liberia. Thomas Buchanan was elected the first governor and a board of directors was named by the parent societies back in the United States.

The Commonwealth of Liberia survived for ten trying years. Diplomatically speaking it was not a nation in any sense. For instance, the newly born commonwealth attempted to impose custom duties on imports, as its only possible source of revenue. Promptly and vehemently the British Government protested. The United States, abetted by the American Colonization Society, intervened warily on behalf of the hard-pressed commonwealth. The Secretary of State, Daniel Webster, reminded the British Government that, "founded principally with a view to the amelioration of the condition of an interesting portion of the great human family, this colony has conciliated more and more the good will and has from time to time received the support of this government."

During 1843, Webster added:

". . . .For several years Liberia was compelled to defend itself by arms and unaided against the native tribes, and succeeded in sustaining itself only at a melancholy sacrifice of comfort and a lamentable loss of human lives. It is due to Her Majesty's government that I should inform you that this government regards Liberia as possessing peculiar claims to the friendly consideration of all Christian powers; that this government will be at all times prepared to interpose its good offices to prevent any encroachment by the colony upon any just right of any nation; and that the United States would be very unwilling to see [Liberia] despoiled of its territory rightfully acquired, or improperly restrained in the exercise of its necessary rights and powers as an independent settlement."

That was straight talk designed to explain American regard for the struggling colony of freed slaves. But obviously Her Majesty's Government were not greatly impressed by Mr. Webster's defense of the sovereign rights of the independent settlement which the United States "felt deeply" about and did so little to support. The parent Colonization Societies conveyed their properties to the Liberia Commonwealth Council, and advised the colonists to declare themselves independent and set up a constitutional government. So the Republic of Liberia was formally born on July 26, 1847. It adopted a constitution generally modeled on that of the United States, and set up an assembly and a judiciary of the same order. Ten years later the colony of Maryland in Liberia came into the new republic as Maryland County.

Paradoxically, Great Britain and several other powers promptly recognized the Republic of Liberia as a sovereign nation, and within two years after its founding the new republic had negotiated commercial treaties with Great Britain, Belgium, Denmark, France, and the Hanseatic republics, but *not* the United States.

In any case a new member had been added to the family of nations. Liberia restricted citizenship and property rights to peoples of "African blood." The new nation's flag, with alternating red and white stripes and a blue field with one white star, supplemented the nation's official motto "The Love of Liberty Brought Us Here."

Americans can hardly take deep pride in the fact that the U.S. Government did not formally recognize Liberia for fifteen years after its founding—not until June 3, 1862, when a tardy Act of Congress under the presidency of Abraham Lincoln simultaneously recognized the two Negro republics of Liberia and Haiti. Earlier a succession of slavery-jittery Congresses had thwarted all efforts to recognize any Negro republic from fear of "political repercussions."

It was March 11, 1863 when the first United States commissioner and consul general to Liberia, John J. Henry of Delaware, was commissioned. On October 21, the first formal treaty of commerce and navigation was signed in London between the United States and Liberia. That treaty included an article which promised that the United States, unless solicited by the Government of Liberia, "engages never to interfere" in the "affairs" between the "aboriginal inhabitants" and the government of the Republic of Liberia. Significantly, the Government of Liberia has never appealed to the United States for aid or intervention in dealing with the native tribes.

The original boundaries of Liberia, as based on concessions procured from chiefs or councils of the native tribes, extended from Cape Mount on the northwest to the San Pedro River on the southeast, with additional purchases of land effected during 1852. By 1866 Great Britain claimed the latter purchases as homestead sites for British African subjects. Liberia protested helplessly, and on November 11,

1885 signed a treaty with Great Britain fixing the Mano River as the northwest boundary. In south and east Liberia, owing in some part to the vagueness of concessions made by native chiefs to the territory called "Maryland in Liberia," the French claimed the San Pedro Valley as Ivory Coast territory. At the instance of the Liberian Government, the American Secretary of State appealed to France to compromise the action. French diplomacy bowed politely and French colonists continued to take over the territory between the San Pedro and the Cavally rivers. In support of her claim, France submitted treaties with native chiefs dated 56 years after the Liberian treaty documents which were first accredited in 1834. Diplomatic eloquence expended by the United States in Liberia's behalf was of no avail.

Late in 1892, Baron von Stein, Liberia's minister resident in Belgium, hastily concluded with France a treaty that relinquished the greater part of Maryland County to France's Ivory Coast Colony and stipulated that the boundary was to follow the middle of the Cavally River for twenty miles from its mouth, and run thereafter by rivers and along meridians in such a manner as to give France the "entire basin of the Niger." The treaty provided that France pay 25,000 francs as indemnity, but left the entire Franco-Liberian boundary still indefinite. This, in turn, led promptly and not at all subtly to France's next grab for Liberian territory. During 1907 Liberia accepted "for peace's sake" a definite and charted inland boundary that gave to the French colony about one-fourth of all Liberia, including a great deal of its richest land.

The dilemma was outlined accurately by President William Howard Taft's message to Congress quoted earlier in this chapter:

". . . .It is from this condition of the interior boundaries of Liberia that her present troubles and embarrassments are largely due. The hinterland of Liberia is practically an unknown region. It is unsettled except by the native tribes . . . and by occasional French or British stragglers. Administrative and police protection in those regions is practically beyond the power of the government at Monrovia, while on the other hand Great Britain and France are alike insistent upon holding Liberia responsible for the safety of their nationals.

"In view of these conditions Great Britain constrained Liberia to conclude the arrangement by which the frontier police of Liberia could be officered by British subjects; on the other hand France claims the right to establish posts for the protection of the French settlers in Liberian territory when the local power is insufficient. Of course, a boundary of indefinite character thus overpassed becomes no boundary, and the claim of the other party elastically moves inward to keep pace with the stragglers. . . ."

As the first decade of the twentieth century ended, Liberia, having stood gallantly for sixty-three years against the vast jungle of West Africa, was still virtually alone facing the more dangerous jungle of power politics.

In the world at large the days of outright slavery were ended. The once powerful American Colonization Societies of the United States had turned to other causes or passed into oblivion. To the United States as a whole, Africa was little known and remote. A few hundred American missionaries were serving in Africa, in many instances at the hazard of their health and lives, and of these a few dozen were in Liberia. But to most of our people Liberia was as vague as the rest of Africa. School texts sometimes inserted brief paragraphs to describe the first republic of the second largest continent in oversimplified generalities.

Occasional roving journalists came to Monrovia, and, less frequently, to other Liberian seafront communities, but they rarely ventured into the interior. Since there were no trains there could be no train-window reporting, and most of the transient reporters learned about Liberia from a brief acquaintance with the Monrovia of legation gossip and gin-and-bitters. Repeatedly the Liberians were amazed and humiliated by what they read about themselves. Poor interpretation abroad aggravated the many difficulties at home. With the coming of the twentieth century the country's struggle for survival became even more desperate. British colonies were gulping Liberian territory from the north and west, while French colonies grabbed from the south and east. As West Africa "opened to trade," the republic was faced both with territorial annihilation and with crucial problems in internal finance and territorial policing.

Although by 1910 there had been a succession of financial crises, Liberia had never been bankrupt, and its national debt of 1.3 million dollars remained insignificant in terms of the resources that could repay the debt. On the whole self-government had succeeded, and the diverse population of native tribesmen, freed slaves and their descendants, and incidental immigrants were living in peace. Faults and weaknesses of many kinds persisted; yet, however impeded and harassed, Liberia was slowly advancing. Missions and mission schools, the first public schools, and courts and churches were being built and put into use. All these were too small and too poor, but the men and women of Liberia were striving.

The nation's most formidable problems were international. Liberia had to protect the integrity of its frontiers in the face of aggressions which it could counteract only by oral or written appeals to justice. It had to police remote inland frontiers, hoping vainly to deprive British and French interests of excuses for taking additional Liberian territory as penalty for alleged injuries resulting from depredations. It confronted the problem of building up national credit to meet foreign obligations and thereby ward off further aggressive actions from without. It needed to provide roads and communication so that the people and products of the great backcountry could reach foreign markets.

The losses already sustained were extremely serious. Between 1847 and 1910 Liberia had lost 44 percent of her original territory. French forces still camped in the Cavally lands. By the Treaty of 1885 the republic had forfeited, literally at cannon's mouth, valuable coastal lands to Britain's Sierra Leone. Again in 1904, when border tribesmen had clashed with British troops in Kanre Lahun in the then northwest corner of Liberia, officials at Monrovia had permitted British forces to enter Liberian territory to "restore order." The hostile chiefs withdrew, but the British stayed.

On October 6, 1909, the Taft Commission, "appointed to investigate the interests of the United States and its citizens in the Republic of Liberia," bluntly reported:

> ". . . It makes little difference whether Great Britain is the upper or the nether millstone. Liberia is between the two and it is the conviction of the commission that unless she has the support of some power commensurate in strength with Great Britain or France she will as an independent power speedily disappear from the map . . ."

During 1908 Liberia had instituted a frontier police force, generally resembling the Philippine Constabulary, to maintain order among the interior tribes whose territories were still largely independent of national boundaries, real or claimed. The first commandant of the Frontier Force had been a British militia officer, Captain R. Mackay Cadell, a

officials, the experiment has turned out disastrously. . . .

"In recent years the attitude of France toward Liberia has hardly been disguised under forms of friendship. She has shown herself disposed to push her boundaries remorselessly into Liberian territory, and has used every available pretext to that end. Her interest in Liberia is apparently that of an heir expectant. . . . If Liberia is to be dismembered, France wants a share of it. In view of this situation the Liberians fully realize that to invite at this juncture the aid of France in the accomplishment of the reforms which have been postponed, but not abandoned, would be to leap from the frying pan into the fire.

"With Germany the relations of Liberia have in recent years not been marred by any of those conflicts which ruffle the waters of international friendship. In Liberia's differences with her neighbors, Germany has lent her at least a sympathetic understanding. For the time being at least, Germany seems to have renounced any idea she may once have had of gaining a foothold in Liberian territory. . . . But if Germany has no immediate territorial interest in Liberia, it has ambitious designs in Africa. . . .

"Liberia is thus confronted by the fact that she can not, without serious danger, call to her aid either Great Britain, France, or Germany. Two of these powers she deeply distrusts, and each of them distrusts the other two. . . . The logic of the situation in the minds of the Liberians points therefore to the United States as the only country which can give them effective aid. Of all Liberia's friends she alone is open to no suspicion of ulterior designs upon Liberia, and alone can give assurance to Great Britain and France and Germany that the legitimate interests of those countries in Liberia, whatever they may be, will not be placed in jeopardy by her actions. . . ."

As U.S. Commissioners to Liberia, Messrs. Roland P. Falkner, George Sale, and Emmett J. Scott late in 1909 presented to the Congress of the United States several significant recommendations made by the Liberian Government. They included the request that the Government of the United States guarantee "as far as practicable" the independence and integrity of Liberia, either alone or in conjunction with certain European powers, and advise and counsel the Government of Liberia on international affairs. Also that the United States Government provide the Government of Liberia with experts in education, finance, military training, agronomy, medicine, and other essential services—at the expense of Liberia, in order to "facilitate and carry out the necessary reforms."

Also that the Government of the United States use its "good offices" to induce American capitalists to establish a bank in Liberia for receiving and disbursing the public revenues, and for building railways and other improvements. Further, that the Government of the United States enter into an arbitration treaty with Liberia, and "use its good and kind offices with the European powers interested in West Africa to enter into similar engagements" with Liberia.

The Liberian Government suggested, too, that the Government of the United States undertake scientific research in Liberia to ascertain more accurately the mineral, agricultural, and other resources of the nation, and to interest American capitalists in their development. It asked that the United States assist Liberia in establishing a school for scientific medical research "with particular reference to the study of tropical diseases." It suggested that the United States help the Government of Liberia in establishing industrial schools that might help "render the Republic self-reliant." And it requested that the United States supervise the organization of a Liberian police and frontier force under American officers and "encourage" a regular steamship service, operated by an American company, to carry mail, passengers, and cargo between America and Liberia, as well as African products to the American markets.

With candor and considerable courage, President Taft's Commissioners and the Secretary of State urged that the United States extend greater and more forthright assistance to Liberia. Secretary Root had earlier addressed President Taft: "It is unnecessary to argue that the duty of the United States toward the unfortunate victims of the slave trade was not completely performed by landing them upon the coast of Africa and that our nation rests under the highest obligations to assist them, so far as they need assistance, toward the maintenance of free, orderly and prosperous civil society. . . ." *

As time and history were shortly to prove, that statement of moral conviction, and the far more explicit report and recommendations of the Taft Commission, were important international documents. The commission recommended that the United States extend its moral and, where necessary, financial aid to Liberia for the prompt settlement of boundary disputes. The Commissioners further urged that the United States "should enable Liberia to refund its debt by assuming as a guarantee for the payment of obligations under such arrangement the control and collection of Liberian customs . . . with the latter's consent." Further, that the United States should assign Army officers or high-ranking noncommissioned officers to organize and drill an "adequate constabulary or frontier police force," and finally that the United States establish and maintain a general research station in Liberia "to investigate plant, mineral

*The Secretary of State—Official Letter, Jan. 18, 1909.

and human resources of the country"; to record the climate, map the topography, and study the causes, treatment, and cure of tropical diseases.

Only a few of the recommendations of the Liberian Government and the observant Commissioners became realities, and those few were greatly modified. More or less in keeping with the Commission's suggestions, a group of American bankers, with British, French, and German associates, and acting with the approval of their respective governments, arranged for Liberia a refunding gold loan of $1,700,000 and with the approval of the Liberian Government placed the control of customs and other assigned revenues in international receivership, with an American agent in charge.

The arrangement was hardly so happy for Liberia as for the international bankers, but at least Liberia found the establishment of a conventional status of credit was to her advantage. She was no longer in danger of having a rich slice of her territory seized by a foreign power every time it was alleged that Chief Woo Woo had failed to pay those nineteen shillings to Sir Lucifer Quashtrap's Number One Boy. Also, after due delay, the United States lent a handful of Negro soldiers to help organize and lead Liberia's military, a venture that was far from a complete success.

Yet despite all its trials and storms and disappointments, by the end of the year 1910 Liberia had passed its most severe test, still a sovereign government. At long last, too, the United States, strongest of all republics, was committed more or less specifically to moral comradeship with the one African republic.

Chapter Three

Liberia Today

YOU LEARN about Liberia slowly, by an almost infinite sequence of impressions, from seeing its vivid dark-green hills, from feeling its hot wet breath and the white fury of its rain, or listening to its many-voiced drums. You learn about Liberia by the gradual process of absorbing small details, all part of a pattern that has more and more significance the better it is known.

You may be walking down a country trail in the late afternoon. You pass a native woman dressed in a gay red robe. On her head she carries a kerosene lantern in preparation for the night that will presently come from the giant forests. You walk over a bridge made of barkless poles bound with fibrous creepers and worn slippery by the passing of countless feet. You notice a native postman with his mail pouch and his water jug balanced evenly on his head. You pass a native village and notice women working before their thatch-topped cones of houses. They bend at the hips while beating the day's supply of rice with wooden pestles.

You may notice a young hunter clad in a white cotton singlet busily peddling antelope meat or exhibiting a baby leopard newly captured from the farther bush. You notice food pots being seasoned with immense helpings of pepper, and you see families eating their one meal of the day. From the next village you hear drums. You hear them and you also feel their vibrations. Presently you make out dark lines of dancers who seem to move like dangling puppets.

As the day passes you begin to appreciate the miraculous variety of this strip of earth and seafront. For instance you may see some of the many still unnamed flowers of the land.

Liberia is the home of the brilliant hibiscus, of the stately green traveler's palm, of the lusty, dark-blue African violets. There are also climbing violets, and thunbergias, fast-growing vines that bear blossoms ranging from pale blue to mauve. You may see the antigonon, misnamed "Honolulu creeper," a tendriled vine with masses of bright pink flowers that climbs on arbors, pergolas, walls, stumps, or sometimes huge forest trees. There is the quisqualis, a semi-climbing perennial shrub with heart-shaped flowers that range in color from pale pink to deep crimson. The West African moonflower, or bonanox, is a perennial climber with stately, silvery white flowers which open late in the evening and close early in the morning. And you may see the haemanthus, a magnificent shrub that bears great scarlet balls of flowers rising from fragile red-flecked stems.

What you see and what you hear are likely at first to impress you as being the stuff of dreams. Weeks or months or years later they still do. Nobody can trust the veracity of any man who says he "knows *all* about Liberia." He does not and cannot. Nevertheless, it is informative to listen to white men in African places: men like the good Swiss trader, Charlie Ramus of Cape Palmas – "Missa Charlie," the piassava-fiber king of West Africa. Or it may be Citizen Maschevieux of near-by French Guinea, founder and leader of a jungle coöperative that markets crops and sells seeds to the far-scattered tribe members. Or Dr. George W. Harley, the founder and for thirty years the director of the great backwoods medical mission at Ganta.

White men who have found places in frontiers of tropical Africa can and do interpret Africa's ways. At nightfall you are likely to return to the screened porch of a plantation house where white men are talking:

"No, sir, these natives don't want white man's ventilation. They loathe and fear drafts. They want to crowd into their huts at night because they fear the leopards more than they fear the disease germs that are real killers . . ."

A doctor answers a question: "No, sir, hereabouts you rarely see knife or bolo wounds or other mayhem. Practically no crimes of violence. . . . Wife-beating? Well, I'd say common enough but not serious. Always plenty of woman palaver, here the same as everywhere else."

There is inevitable talk about food and eating and drinking; talk that frequently begins and usually ends with the subject of Liberian "country chop." Country chop is as African as the Poro school, or the country devil, or the thundermist, or that bird-lover's nightmare the hornbill. And country chops are almost never precisely the same, a fact that adds greatly to their appeal.

Country chop is a tradition of eating. You begin by taking a plate or an earthen bowl and perhaps a napkin and a knife, fork, and spoon if you have to be fussy. Depending somewhat on taste and company, you begin by smearing your plate with shredded pepper—the oily green pepper that is violently hot. It is highly advisable to smear with your knife. If you use your spoon or fork to spread the pepper and use the same utensil in eating, you are practically certain to get your mouth and tongue painfully burned.

Forgetting such trivial hazards, you begin by filling your plate with rice—tender, well-cooked native rice with the hulls left on. Over the fluffy mound of rice you pour palm-nut gravy, which is dark brown, exquisitely rich in flavor, and formidably fattening. Then you spread on the meat—the shredded roast chicken or chicken legs or antelope or venison or smoked fish, or (just possibly) elephant meat. All this you cover with thick and successive spreadings of shredded coconuts, roasted peanuts, thin slices of ripe banana, and sizable slices of the unmatchably sweet pineapples of Africa. Next you add one or more of the side embellishments: sweet pickles, ripe or stuffed olives, preserved citron, watermelon rind, or the Liberian "butter pear" which makes all other avocados seem insipid.

Then, speaking little and thinking not at all of your waistline, you eat. Deliberately you refill your plate and drink—cold water, or tea, or hot coffee, or cold highballs, or iced beer depending on place and choice, and then you eat again. Then you meditate on a reasonably cool and quiet place in which to sleep. You rise slowly, and relying on considerable support from the chairs, shrubs, or people en route you proceed to lie down.

When you wake you are likely to believe—or at least to feel—a great deal more about Liberia. The characteristic fare of a nation reveals its moods and artistries as does nothing else.

Another of the things you are sure to become acutely conscious of in Liberia is the drumming. In practically any populated area of the interior you will hear drums. During my first month inland I listened to drums on twenty-six nights. And like most newcomers, I began to ponder the meaning of African drums. I confided my interest to a tribe boy who was swinging an ax and thereby gradually making small bits of wood somewhat smaller. The boy smiled, exhibiting a stunning set of white teeth, and admitted that he himself was a singer (that is, a drummer) and that he knew all the beats. My enthusiasm for people who know all the beats is either unbounded or absolutely nonexistent. In this case it was the former.

The ax boy vanished into the bush and presently returned with a leather-headed drum about the size and shape of a half-gallon lard bucket. He squeezed it with his left elbow and began drumming with the fingers and heel of his right hand. "Drum talk sweet," he said. "Now drum tell somebody daid. . . . Now a lil' babee comes. . . . Now a hunter gets meat. Here," he added, "come woman palaver . . . new woman . . . old woman . . . fat woman . . . new girl. . . . Drum say come eat rice. . . . Drum say go hide. . . . Stranger folks come here. . . ." The instructor grinned again and his fingers leaped playfully. "Dance time comes. . . . War dance . . . tribe dance . . . woman dance." His smile faded and the cadence diminished "Drum get mad. . . . Drum talk mean." Then the informant's frown faded and his smile became angelic. "Now drum talk sweet . . . some more. . . ."

Drums set the tempo of a Liberian music which is distinctive of the land yet rich in contrasts. At state functions in Monrovia, the seaport capital, officials and guests frequently "lead in" with a "grand march" followed with the Virginia reel or an attractive quadrille. Then eighteenth-century Virginia or seventeenth-century Paris shifts to today's American variants of the foxtrot, waltz, or rhumba.

Liberia sings, as a rule too shrilly for comfort, in churches and concert halls. But on the capital streets one hears the songs of the Congo immigrants: magnificent choral singing, much imitated here in the United States. And along the waterfronts of Monrovia and other port towns you sometimes hear the superb chanting of the Krus and other tribes of boatmen. I have heard a close harmony rising from three different canoes, at least fifty yards apart. The singing, in good pitch and rhythm, was in three different tribal languages of Liberia, but the improvised harmony was excellent.

Among the tribespeople, music, like dancing, is more than recreation. It is a way and a part of life. A boy working far from home and among strange people picks up an empty bucket or an abandoned gasoline tin and makes himself a drum. Or he hollows out a piece of wood, stretches a goatskin over it, places strings of piassava fibers, and there he has a guitar. Tribespeople—men, women, and children alike—work, play, row, dance, and tramp to the rhythm of songs and chants. Their music simply will not be stilled. For them it is breath, the sequence of the days, the swing of an ax, the beat of a hoe, the churning of a rice pestle, the sweep of a blacksmith's hammer. There is rarely a hut or a family without its own particular musician, without its own improvisations of musical instruments—homemade guitars, rattles, bells, or xylophones. These last are made of from four to ten hand-carved softwood "keys" laid and pegged across the trunks of banana stalks and beaten with softwood mallets. But most important and most numerous are the drums, with their magic of moods and contrasts.

Contrast is the rule of the land, contrast of remarkable scope and variety. After viewing a devil-dance in a tribe village you may pick up a belated weekly newspaper published at Monrovia, only a few miles away, and read such items as these:

> The Honourable the Vice-President of Liberia and chairman of the Liberian Delegation to the United Nations Peace and Security Conference at San Francisco, California, U.S.A., will deliver an address in Cox Memorial Auditorium under the distinguished patronage of His Excellency the President of Liberia.

Or:

This year's graduating class of the College of West Africa [Monrovia] includes Lucretia Sherman, valedictorian; Joseph Richards, salutatorian; Joseph Jenkins Peal, Jacob Armah Jones, Isabel Karnga, Charles Emmet Cooper, George W. A. Knuckles, Mabel E. Fagans, Lawrence K. Gbuie, Amos T. Nagbe, Sophronice C. Richards, Joshua J. Ross, and Solomon W. Tumu.*

Monrovia, the ocean-front capital, is in many ways a paradox. It is a tin-roofed tropical town with countless unfinished dwellings and yet one of the most strategic and important African seaports. It is both an African and a world crossroads, as well as the best doorway to the vastness of West Africa. It has a unique internationalism of people and goods: Moslem dress, formal English and American styles, African traders in gold and scarlet robes, portable phonographs, radios, and American-African music—spirituals, blues, the Charleston, and comedy records. The town's stores display merchandise from many lands: Manchester prints, dried fish, American soaps, bolt goods, and ready-mades in addition to native products, imported colored sodas, sardines and canned salmon, woolen caps with tassels, and curls of strong leaf tobacco.

Monrovia is the capital of a Negro nation and has long since ceased to declaim about it. One senses this in the current administration of the Liberian government. When the Liberian delegation (the Vice President and Secretary of State) arrived at San Francisco they were met by an expectant group of editorial lobbyists representing some of the radical Negro press and the Communist press of the United States. The Liberian representatives spoke to their

---

*Items quoted from the *Weekly Mirror*, Monrovia, Vol. 16, No. 46, Nov. 16, 1945.

interviewers precisely as they would have spoken had they been at home: "We are here to represent a nation—not a race."

The tenet that Liberia is a nation, not a cause or a rallying point, is clearly confirmed by the attitude and actions of the government. Under its present government, Liberia is financially solvent. Both its external and internal debts are steadily diminishing. For more than fifteen years no new debts have been acquired. The one bank (Bank of Monrovia) has a strong financial position and adequately serves the needs of the community. The bank's debt losses average below one-fourth of one percent.

These are details but they nevertheless help in bringing the important first impressions of Liberia into focus. Recently I thought of all this while listening to the state-of-the-nation address of William V. S. Tubman, since 1944 the President of Liberia.

Mr. Tubman, an attractive and immensely sincere preacher-and-lawyer, Liberian-born graduate of a mission school, was making his address to the third session of Liberia's fortieth legislature.

He began by outlining in considerable detail his own conceptions of the world situation and the dilemmas of peace. He announced the reëstablishment of Liberian consulates in New York and Liverpool, the restoration of the Liberian legation in Paris, and the prospective establishment of diplomatic relations with Russia, Chile, and Lebanon. He reported a substantial excess of treasury receipts over government expenditure, the continued reduction of the external and internal debt of Liberia, and his country's excellent prospects for shortly becoming the world's only debt-free nation. He requested legislation to prohibit gambling, which he marked as being on the increase in West

Africa generally. He asked for far-reaching reforms in prison administration and for legislation requiring a health certificate from a qualified physician as a requisite for marriage. He then proposed the reduction of the Liberian Frontier Force, in view of better relations among the interior tribes, and commended the Liberian militia for its efficiency.

The President pointed out that increasing numbers of tribal chiefs are asking for more adequate medical facilities and that their applications must have a prominent place in government plans. He requested the repeal of the prevailing big-game license (costing $250 a year) so that tribespeople might better defend their rice crops from depredation by wild elephants. He noted that by virtue of a recent referendum a constitutional amendment had been enacted to extend suffrage to all Liberian tribesmen who paid hut taxes. He recommended an additional amendment to extend suffrage to all Liberian women, tribe members or non-tribe members, who pay property taxes.

He called for legislation to authorize and effect an official census, and to procure free schoolbooks for distribution to public schools; for a 50-percent increase in foreign scholarships to be granted Liberian youth by the Liberian government; and for increased government support of technical high schools. He urged increased government appropriations for public education and health administration, and also the continuation of efforts to effect better diversification of crops so that Liberia may be better assured of self-sufficiency during the years ahead.

The President spoke to a crowded assembly room on a hot African afternoon. His theme and the direction of his logic were markedly like those of a recent liberal President of the United States and several liberal Governors, but what he said had evidently to be appraised differently. He was speaking to a nation made up mostly of communal tribes; the overwhelming majority of Liberians consist of twenty-three different tribes as a whole or in part. The need to coördinate the national and the tribal governments is thus unique among contemporary democracies.

As one practical instance of this need, a few years ago a failure of the life-sustaining rice crop brought famine to several areas of inland Liberia. The famine spread over the Tchien area. In the lands about Kunobo, tribespeople were reported to have died of starvation. Normally productive farming centers, such as the Webbo districts, were almost deserted by the distressed tribespeople. Then, early the following year (1944), the Liberian Government through its Interior Department began urging and helping the tribespeople to double their rice acreages as a safeguard against a repetition of the famine. These efforts were encouragingly successful; miles of new rice clearings appeared along various jungle trails and in new jungle clearings. And by the following Independence Day (July 26) the critical situation was on the mend. Moreover, from far-scattered inland points there began to appear canoe or headpack loads of incidental crops — cabbage, peppers, squash, eggplant, and corn. The efforts of a central and elected government helped effect the turn.

The Tubman administration works particularly hard and well to serve the relatively inaccessible interior which is the home of all the more populous tribes. Shortly after his inauguration, the President instituted a continuing series of official "palavers" among the tribes in their home villages. As a beginning Tubman and his official party traveled inland to attend the Salala Conference of Chiefs, a recurrent assembly of paramount chiefs, clan chiefs, elders, and other tribe members of the central provinces.

The first palaver lasted for ten days. Repeatedly chiefs complained that individual or non-tribe citizens had been claiming or occupying large tracts of farming lands that belonged to the tribes and were essential to their survival. The President proceeded to establish clear precedents for confirming and enforcing tribal title to agricultural lands. The issue was vital. The requirements of tribe survival require a plot of at least twenty-five acres for the use of each family within the tribe, and customarily one-fourth of the collective acreage for use as "strangers' farms." And twenty-five acres to a family is a minimum figure. In each planting season a family clears, burns, and plants a new rice field and permits the previous year's yield to return to jungle. It is the ancient routine of allowing fallow land for eventual reclaiming.

The Tubman administration proceeded to state and enforce a policy of respecting priority in the occupancy of land by a given tribe. Politically such a feat is never easy. But to equatorial Africa the tribe is indispensable and without the tribes there could be no Liberia.

The official palavers of the President, his cabinet members, and other officials, with and among the inland tribes and chiefdoms are helping the chiefs show their competency as leaders. Palaver records prove the point. As one example, at the President's first palaver, Paramount Chief Boto Barclay urged that the Liberian government appropriate larger sums for roads and bridges and technical help so that the interior chiefs could better employ their own tribesmen to open more roads and trade routes to the sea. He explained, too, that his people are eager to build and maintain more public schools for tribe youths—"making all necessary provision for good light and free ventilation as well as taking precautions against drafts."

Chief Boto stressed the eagerness of his tribesmen to improve their farming practices. He urged reform in harvest techniques. "Many inland people dry their rice on the bare earth, thus contaminating it with rocks and mud. . . . Government should make it compulsory for producers to dry their rice on mats or some other material that prevents the rice from coming into contact with the ground."

Repeatedly the palavers have stressed the needs for more diversified crops and for better shipping facilities on the rivers as well as on the seacoast. They stress the dangers of open-sea navigation in native boats, the advantages of operating motor-driven launches in place of dugout canoes, and hundreds of other needs and problems which, however minor they may seem to the outsider, are essential considerations in Liberia.

The palaver is a rudimentary legislature. It is also an African version of the New England town meetin'. It is characterized by the timeless generosity of jungle African etiquette, by its kindliness, its meditative, amiable stubbornness. The "dash" or gift to the visitor remains orthodox: an egg or several eggs, a pineapple, a cup of rice, a piece or a bolt of cloth, or a chicken. Recently Liberia's President accepted gratefully a cow as a "dash" from a rural chief. Promptly and insistently he "dashed" the chief fifty dollars in return.

At the palaver one senses the orthodoxy of authority on the basis of which the tribal structure of the country is built. Authority begins in the family with the "head woman" or first wife, and then moves upward to the husband or family head, above whom are the tribe elders. Next is the town chief—in larger villages the half-chiefs or quarter-chiefs, then the clan chief, and last the paramount chief. Responsibility then passes to the district commissioner, the supervising commissioner, the Secretary of Interior (all appointed by the President), and finally to the President of Liberia, who is ex-officio the chief of all the chiefs. In a sense this is democracy within democracy.

In Liberia the tribal chief, whether petty or paramount, is not a king, but is, in effect, an elected official. Usually he has qualities of natural leadership and he may be a chief's son, though often he is a commoner. Not infrequently the clan chiefs, and in rare cases the paramount chiefs, are women. The powers of the chiefs vary considerably with individuals and tribes. Some chiefs are dominating; others are strongly influenced, if not actually led, by the tribe's council of elders. Occasionally a chief is sadistic, tyrannical, or greedy, and a few chiefs have sought to establish themselves as kings. But the fact remains that the "chieftaincy" is not a throne. Any chief can be deposed by his followers. Many have been. In Liberia the word is "sacked."

But the chief is a leader, a shepherd, and a magistrate, the administrator of an indigenous system of laws and folkways born of a communal people who are not inclined toward violent crimes. The tribal court, an open-forum palaver, is the age-old bar (or mat) of justice. Woman palaver and debt palaver are far and away the most frequent docket items; petty thefts a weak third. As a rule woman palaver in inland Liberia is extremely detailed. Frequently the testimony long predates the subject's birth, with elaborate recitations of how the claimant or husband presented the expectant mother-in-law with a bolt of cloth or a basket of rice, thereby establishing the proposition that the woman was spoken for, many moons before she was actually born;

or how her heart or her person had been won long before she came of woman's age.

Usually the chief or the elders who preside at palaver listen with infinite patience, as the cases unfold. Eventually the chief or his elders decide the case, but they can grant the defendant "time to pay," which may be long extended. Flogging is the usual tribe penalty for conviction of theft, though sometimes the punishment is assignment to menial work about the village. In any case, tribal justice requires the approval of the next higher chief or tribe authority. Capital crimes are automatically referred to the district commissioner, an official of the Liberian government. In the principal population centers of the interior, the government stations salaried magistrates who conduct the courts that issue writs of arrest (delivered by a duly authorized constable or bondsman) and warrants of search. The home is inviolate, a man's castle, even if the home is nothing more than a mat of straw or a spot of smooth earth.

Liberian life is far from simple; its age is infinite; its change is incessant. While large planes roar overhead, the tribespeople continue to bathe in the local creeks using soap made of wood ashes and palm oil molded in round gray balls. On the bypaths one meets remarkable things, such as tall fast-walking snails; oversize salamanders with protruding stubs of eyes; stilt-legged sheep without wool; grotesque forest birds with wings that go *phlop-phlop-phlop* as they fly; black crows with exquisite white bands about their necks. In the interior one still sees bush money—twisted strips of iron about sixteen inches long and shaped like slender T's, smelted locally and drawn into money by the tribal blacksmiths. From twelve to twenty of the iron sticks are worth a shilling or a quarter in exchange. Though officially Liberia now uses United States currency, until recently it used British, and in the interior the value of goods is usually in pence, shillings, or pounds.

The tribal blacksmiths are respected and proficient practitioners of a great craft that is usually handed down from father to son. At Zorzor you may meet two crippled smiths, both victims of infantile paralysis. They are craftsmen and admirable citizens. They crawl about with the help of hand grips and heat their forges with charcoal. For bellows they use tubes made of hide set into low clay walls, and for anvils, blocks of granite. Year after year the crippled smiths of Zorzor carry on their work. The one who speaks English exclaims over the talents of Americans: "Great blacksmiths you got! Think how one man with hammer and anvil he makes the huge big airplane – also the jeeps. . . . Fine – fine blacksmiths!"

Most of the tribespeople enjoy quite distinct professional standings: farmers, merchants, hunters, priests, chiefs, elders, blacksmiths, medicine men, or house builders. Recently I pondered this while talking with Henry Moore, a young African from near-by Sierra Leone. Henry came to Liberia to be foreman of the Firestone brick yards near Harbel. Having proved himself an exceptional leader and executive, he had taken up pottery molding as a hobby. He had begun by shaping and kiln-firing simple crockery and vases. Then he proceeded to more ambitious ornamental pottery, molding conventionalized roosters, pigs, antelope, and other fauna of the countryside, all with charming directness and the delightful quality of African caricature. In time and with practice he began to sculp and cast miniature busts and figures of people. When I visited him he was completing a heroic bust of the President of Liberia, done solely from a newspaper picture of Mr. Tubman. It seemed to me splendid work, with all the distilled folk spirit of centuries of African living. There are a great many Henry Moores in Liberia, and in the rest of Africa. There are a great many like Tobo, the crippled blacksmith of Zorzor.

As the tribespeople reckon time, a year is the interval between the clearing of a new field and the harvest of the planted crop. When they plant two crops during the same calendar year, they count it as two years. This creates a great deal of the Africa-style vagueness regarding dates and ages. The youth who says he is 23, the patriarch who gives his age as 90, and the girl who admits to being 19 are likely to be exaggerating their real ages by at least one-fifth.

In upcountry Liberia the month that we call January is the "big cool moon," a misty month when the desert winds called harmattans blow down from the vast north. They are drying winds, lowering the customarily high humidity and producing the effect, if not the reality, of coolness. What we call February is also a "cool moon." March is the "sick moon," partly because food supplies of the previous year are running low; the tribesman's fare is frequently poor and the chances of getting sick are thereby enhanced. April also is a "sick moon," a period of rice planting that is often a month of even leaner larders, and still more malaria and such waterborne diseases as dysentery.

May, June, and July are "wet moons," during which the great rains begin and continue night after night. August, also a wet moon, in Mano country is called *Boyo,* "hungry time"; the new rice is still not ready for harvest, and too frequently the old rice is already eaten. September is the "rice-cutting moon." But the rice is often late and accordingly, in many tribal lands September is labeled "the moon when many chickens starve." October, usually a relatively dry month with a mere three to eight inches of rainfall, is called "big rice-cutting moon," and less optimistically "the moon with no water in the house." As the month of transition from the long rainy season (or winter) to the comparatively short dry season (or summer), October is also the time for small-garden planting. November is the "small rice-cutting moon." It sees the rice harvest brought to a close, and it sees the hunting season rise to a climax. December is the "small cold moon," the time of *wallow wallow,* the big rain drops of the occasional passing showers.

When time for rice-planting comes, tribal townspeoples and villagers move out to clear and plant the land. Tree- and bush-felling is man's work. Where the soil is good the same clearing can be planted to crops for two successive years; where thin, one year is the limit. With the harvest made, the land is returned to fallow for three to seven years, during which time the greedy jungle growths quickly take over.

Clearing the "bush," which includes felling trees ten feet or more in girth, is extremely hard work. It begins with bush-chopping, swinging homemade iron knives or sharp cutlasses to clear away the undergrowth. That done, the tree-fellers move in. Usually they wear *zewolos,* leather work gloves made of antelope or other skins, and little else. Armed with narrow axes with cutting edges no more than an inch or an inch and a half wide, axes mounted on club-like wooden handles about twenty inches long, strong men then chop and fell the big trees, accompanied as a rule by the pounding of drums or gasoline tins.

"Farm-cutting" is proud work. With each successive season the clan or the town names its champion bush-cutter, who is frequently honored with a crested helmet, or a leather collar, or some other token of reward and respect. The tree-fellers usually work in groups of from ten to thirty or forty men; sometimes the felling line is a hundred men long or more. Oftentimes an entertainer stays with each group, an adaptable clown who pounds drums in the tempo for chopping, chants the virtues of the strong men, ridicules the lazy, and seeks to keep the work in motion. As land is cleared, the chief or the medicine man tests the soil and gives his opinions, frequently expert, of its desirability as a farming site.

When the razing is completed and the drying winds parch the leaves, the felled bush is pulled into windrows ready for fire and the "fire-swingers" wait for the signal to go. When the chief or headman gives the signal, the fire-swingers move across the felling in a widely spaced line, all bearing blazing fagots or bamboo torches with which they set fire to the future fields. Frequently the highly ceremonious burning "bees" turn to hunting bees. As fire sweeps over the dead bush, small animals such as hares, squirrels, and fieldmice scurry to save themselves from the fire. Men, women, and youths alike plunge after the "small-small" refugees and bag them as "small beef."

When the burning is finished the women and girls of the village join their men to begin the planting quickly before rain can wash away the ashes that provide valuable plant food. During the planting season each sunup sees an exodus from the villages to the farms, which are frequently located several miles away. By sunup at latest the able-bodied men, women, boys, and girls set out along the trails that lead to their little fields. Usually they travel in small amiable clusters, talking and laughing, indulging in mimicry and repartee punctuated by occasional dance steps.

The younger women carry their babies tied in the back folds of their dresses or tunics, while the young children play alongside. Breakfast, if there is any, is a brief interval of pot-raiding, of nibbling or gobbling whatever was left over from the previous day's meal. If the rice stores have been exhausted to provide seed for the new planting, the penalty is hard work on empty stomachs.

Planting the rice is primarily woman's work, though the men and boys usually help in one way or another such as clearing away the charred limbs and tree trunks left by the fire, or pounding drums, or chanting to encourage the women at their work.

Sometimes, particularly in the case of the poorer tribesmen, men and their wives work together to plant the rice. The richer men and chiefs of the tribe assign their many wives to work in groups, sometimes twenty or thirty or more women in one party with the head wife or the oldest woman as boss. Equipped with sharp-pronged sticks, or narrow-bladed hoes, sometimes with homemade wooden hoes, the women move into their designated plots. Usually they shed their dresses or robes if they are wearing any, cache them in some sheltered spot, and work naked or in abbreviated girdles of tree bark or raffia leaves.

The actual proprietorship of any field or plot is puzzling to the outside observer. It would probably drive an American land lawyer raving mad. The planting is basically communal. Usually the family farms cover somewhere between one and three acres. Chiefs or tribesmen with several wives and still more children often require fields of twenty to forty acres, depending on the abundance or the scarcity of the lands available for the tribe's use.

Usually the tribeswomen sow the rice broadside, taking the seed from jugs which they have toted to the fields on their heads. Having sown the seed, they cover the sowing with their miniature hoes, or rake soil over the grains with cutlasses and switches. Or sometimes they plant the grains directly into shallow holes which they punch with pronged sticks. Such planting is hard work, but it is usually done well and with remarkable good humor.

When afternoon shadows grow long, or when night begins to settle, the chief or "boss man" calls the fields to rest. The field women, drenched with sweat if not with rain, gather up their planting tools, call in their children, slip on their clothes, tie on their babies, set jars or portage baskets on their heads, and so set out for home. On the way they collect firewood or kindling twigs and pluck edible greens or catch snails to add to the evening meal. Back at home they fall to cooking.

However hard the tribe wife works in the planting fields, she works at least as hard to prepare and serve the family's meal. As elsewhere, good cooking is the woman's way of keeping her man's favor, or her equity in or minority share of a man. The one-meal-a-day routine is partly habitual but also, unfortunately, it reveals the chronic shortage of food.

Meat is both scarce and costly and this has much to do with the many diseases and debilities that result from the lack of sufficient proteins. The shortage of meat puts a premium on other foods of rural Liberia, including the African yams, the yellow-skinned sweet potatoes, the long-necked squashes, and the edible luffa, a ground vine that bears a pithy fruit vaguely similar to summer squash. There are also wild-growing eggplants, undersized tomatoes, and many varieties of wild mushrooms.

Plantains, those plump starchy cousins of bananas, are among the most coveted of the native fruits, and perhaps are indigenous to Equatorial West Africa. As a rule the plantains are roasted and eaten like potatoes or boiled and mashed and mixed with the richly flavored palm oil. The ordinary or sweet bananas (*Musa sapiens*) grow well in many parts of Liberia and in remarkable variety including the big yellow Gros Michels which we in the United States usually buy and eat. There are also various types of the Cavendish, a smaller and drier banana, and the Madeira, the fat red banana that many of us ate as children. There are the small, pale yellow, and exquisitely flavored "Lady Finger" bananas, and many unclassified and degenerate species including the soft-pulped "water bananas."

Presumably all the sweet bananas are immigrants to West Africa, as are the sweet-fleshed, green-rind oranges, the oversized green limes or lemons, and the big, exquisitely sweet pineapples. These and several other immigrant crops are now firmly planted in Liberian earth.

But on the whole the tribal farmers are not orchardists. They regard trees as God's palaver, creations and donations by the Great Spirit, whatever His name, and they do little to increase the yield of food-bearing trees.

Interior Liberia has a number of incidental crops, some of which are definitely gaining in dietary importance. Among them is the superb salad green called "palm cabbage," the tender heart buds of the African oil palm eaten raw with palm oil dressing. Other staple greens are the top leaves of the bombax tree, the young tender leaves of the cassava, okra, squash, and sweet potato vines, all of which are boiled in water and then soaked with palm oil and stirred into rice. The fiercely hot capsicums, apparently native to inland Liberia, provide the favorite condiment.

Then there are dishes of local importance, foods and seasonings which though they would not appeal to the American palate, or find a place on the menus of Monrovia or the coastal towns, are nevertheless nutritious. The list includes such protein sources as land terrapin, giant snails, big green grasshoppers, oversize crickets, the fat larvae of palm beetles, and certain types of snakes. Jungle rats are eaten. Termites are lured from the man-high anthills by means of torches, captured, boiled in hot water, spread out in the sun to dry, and eaten like roasted nuts. But such foods vary with tribes and locales. Some tribes, for example, have specific taboos against snakes, alligators, and reptilian life generally, while other tribes eat them eagerly.

In parts of Liberia there is now the beginning of an attempt at crop diversification. The borders of rice paddies are sometimes planted to cotton, okra, squashes, tomatoes, or other vegetables. And frequently after the rice is well sprouted, tiny tobacco plants or the roots of yams and sweet potatoes are slipped into the same earth.

This beginning, however, is still on a very small scale and, first and last, rice is the staple and the balance of the Liberian bill-of-fare. The philosophical old tribesmen who told me that his people grow rice to live and live to grow rice was not being merely aphoristic.

Whatever the place or the crop, vigilance is essential. Crops can be bewitched, but – more important than this – rice and all other crops are too often destroyed by monkeys, wild hogs, forest buffalo, antelope, and (most destructive of all) roving herds of elephants. Newly planted seed and ripened grain alike are at the mercy of the jungle birds, particularly parrots and weavers. The weaver or Liberian rice bird is an attractive songster and the worst menace to rice.

As a protective measure when the village sowing is completed, "guarding away" the birds becomes an essential communal obligation. Usually the young boys make the most effective guards: boys with loud and shrill voices, great energy, and exceptional talent with slingshots. Many boys no more than eight or nine years old can throw pebbles from slingshots as accurately as their elders can shoot bullets from carbines. Frequently they stand guard from first dawn to darkness, and to speed the long hours they frolic, run, shout, and chant throughout most of the day.

Where the ravages by birds are excessive, tribal farmers sometimes build platforms near the center of the field and surround them with taut strings or thongs to which they tie gongs, bells, gourd rattles, tin cans, or any other noisemakers available. Boys then stand on the platform, and throughout the long day they pull the strings. The clang of the noisemakers, added to the swishing of the strings, is effective for scaring away spirits as well as birds. Sometimes dogs are used to supplement the watch – rangy, brown-blotched mongrels that usually move cautiously and seldom bark.

Good fortune, patient guarding, and about five growing months make the rice tall and velvet-green. When the grain heads grow heavy and the home rice pots grow light the harvest is a welcome, often a life-saving, climax. Sometimes the early September rice is plucked while the grain is still milky and soft. This new rice is both a coveted food and a major cause of painful bellyaches.

As the long wet season comes to its end in October, the principal harvests begin. Once more all the women and some of the men move into the rice fields. With considerable formality, working in lines and moving to the beating of drums or the chant of singers, they clip off the waiting grain heads with metal knives, and using fiber or rice-straw binders they shape small bundles, usually only five or six inches long, load them on head baskets, and carry them home for winnowing. The first day's gathering of new rice is usually given away, this being an old African custom, an expression of gratitude. By late October or early

November the big harvest is finished and the farmers' year is ended.

In Liberia the struggle for subsistence is extremely real. It requires the maximum exploitation of the foods that are obtainable from forests, streams, and open lands. Meat, the basic protein food, remains desperately scarce. For reasons that we shall shortly notice in detail, livestock development has been gravely retarded. This means that the forests, jungles, and rivers must continue to provide the greater part of the proteins; that the wild-animal population is still of vital importance to the people.

Speaking generally, antelope, the kindred wild deer, and wild hogs are the readiest native sources of meat, though elephants (which the tribespeople eat virtually in toto, including the skin) are the most coveted of all game. The bush cow or forest buffalo is also highly valued and very dangerous to kill. It is about as big as a medium steer and is equipped with ominous, stubby horns and a uniformly bad disposition. It gives excellent meat and leather, provided the hunter does not come out second-best. Recently the writer met a Vai boy who had been seriously gored by a bush cow; no doubt he would have been killed had he not skinned up a "proper tall" tree. But he had kept his cutlass in his belt, and late on his second night in the tree he slipped down, faced his enemy, and somehow or other managed to slit the bush cow's throat. He carried the animal's head as testimony.

Some of the creeks and rivers abound with fish and many of the swamplands are the homes of eels. So tribespeople, men and women, boys and girls alike, go out to catch fish and eels and the big lobsterlike crayfish for which they set elaborate traps woven of raffia. They spear water frogs and seine for minnows and small fish with homemade scoop nets. They use bamboo and other native canes to build fish weirs and fish corrals. The tribe blacksmiths pound out fishing hooks (which for some reason do not have barbs) and fashion iron-headed spears for spearing or gigging the larger fish. At night lines of giggers wade through the river pools and with almost unbelievable skill spear fish by moonlight or torchlight. During the day women often take time off from their creek-bank washing to bait hooks and set lines for catfish, or to drag home-woven seines through the shallow pools scooping out the minnows. The Krus, Shantis, and other seafaring tribes fish professionally at sea. In all, fishing is immensely important to Liberia and is chronically in need of better development.

Hunting, even more important, is also more honored as a profession. Usually the native hunter of inland Liberia is primarily a trapper, and jungle trapping is a masterpiece of simple but inspired ingenuity. That is a strong assertion. Personally, I have never been able to work even the most elementary of African puzzles, such as the casual ones that call for maneuvering knots and beads. I try; and after hours of bewildered effort and many gin-and-bitters I invariably fail — whereupon the smallest and slowest of the small boys, equipped with only a porcelain smile and a billowy nightshirt, works the puzzle with three deft finger-moves. I grin feebly, pick up the puzzle, try again — and again fail. Whence my unbounded respect for the trapping techniques of the Liberian interior!

The jungle huntsmen are masters with noose traps and deadfalls. I never made a noose trap, though once in my rural Arkansas youth I spent several hours building a deadfall planned to curb the hordes of rats that used to invade the attic and make away with the drying peanut crop. I took a huge oak board, about four inches thick, a foot wide, and fourteen feet long, and propped one end of it with a set of figure-4 triggers carved out of a strip of cedar shingle. I baited the tip of the horizontal trigger with cheese and weighted the deadfall with Chambers' Encyclopædic Dictionary and a hundred-pound bag of block salt.

Late that night the household was awakened by a shattering uproar. A chunk of plaster dropped from the parlor ceiling. My father leaped out of bed and hopped feet-first through the front porch window which he had absent-mindedly closed. My uncle Sam, who slept on the back porch, grabbed his shotgun, fired a warning shot in the dark, then ran like the wind toward the horse barn and entangled himself with the wire clothesline.

I lit a lamp, shinnied up the attic ladder, and set out to locate the flattened remains of the peanut-eating rats. I pushed away the dictionary and the salt bag, lifted the big board, and there beneath it were the completely flattened remains of the smallest mouse I have ever seen. Though flat as blotting paper the cadaver still would not have covered a quarter.

Deadfalls, Liberia style, are different. There is, for example, the leopard deadfall. The trapper suspends the contraption over a pathway that leopards are known to follow. He obstructs the trail with a network of raffia or other light fiber, anticipating that the leopard will raise one paw to clear the path of the impediment. Directly below the flimsy blockade the trapper sets a stiff mat or board panel, on one end of which is a peg trigger. One end of a heavy cord is tied to the trigger; the other end to the long arm of two levers that are supported by notched or forked posts six to eight feet above the path. The short end of the lever holds up a stout loop of vines by which a big log is suspended. When the peg trigger is released by the weight of the leopard's foot on the panel, the balanced levers fly up and the log falls to crush the marauder below.

The spear trap is a variant of the deadfall. A heavy log, with a sharpened end, is suspended by a rope made of fibers or vines from a stout limb that overhangs an animal trail. An end of the rope placed directly across the trail is tied to a peg trigger. The slightest pressure against the rope releases the trigger and so permits the heavy spear to plunge down upon the passing quarry.

The spring-noose trap is also well known in Liberian hunting. The trapper selects a springy small tree or sapling beside a game trail, strips off its top and lower branches, and bending the little tree down binds its top part close to the pathway with a cord set noose-style to one or more pegs. He baits the pegs. When the animal, preferably a wild pig, nibbles the bait, the released end of the sapling springs upright tightening the noose, thus (so the hunter hopes) leaving the catch dangling hopelessly in the air.

The hunters set traps in trees for monkeys or lemurs or porcupines. They set bow traps for birds. They also devise cage traps for leopards, the most destructive and ruthless of all jungle killers, and in Liberia still far too prevalent. The trapper begins by building a stout cage perhaps eight feet long and three to five feet wide. He drives corner stakes into the ground beside a trail that is frequented by leopards, binds the stakes together with vines or leather thongs, and covers the enclosure with a roof built of interwoven branches. Then he places a row of shorter stakes and vine wrappings to divide the cage into one small compartment and one larger one, each with a door or gate.

The door of the larger compartment is held up and open by a cord attached to a set of triggers placed near the inside partition. The hunter takes live bait, usually a goat, and places it in the smaller compartment, which is then securely fastened shut. He leaves the goat without food or water. The goat wails. In theory the strolling leopard, attracted by the plaints of the goat, views the prospect, walks into the big compartment of the cage, and attempts to make his way into the small compartment. In so doing he springs the key trigger, which lets fall the door behind him.

Though somewhat reminiscent of inventions by Rube Goldberg, this cage trap is actually the most effective defense against leopards. The caged leopard roars and threshes. He often gets to the goat, and – if the trap is not strongly built – he is likely to break out, which is never good. As a rule cage traps are placed near the villages and bells or pieces of metal are tied to the cage walls to sound an alarm. When the alarm sounds, the hunter recruits as many helpers as possible and hurries to kill the trapped leopard. This is neither safe nor easy. Suitable guns and ammunition are chronically scarce, and it is a formidable feat to kill a leopard, even a trapped leopard, with spears, rocks, or clubs. One free swipe by a forepaw can rip out a man's intestines, break a leg, or bash in his skull. Few lone hunters survive an encounter with a trapped or a wounded leopard.

That there are still a great many leopards in Liberia is proved by the traffic in leopard skins, claws, and teeth, and the persisting depredations of the jungle cats. With the best of reasons all tribespeople dread them. Accordingly the successful leopard trapper becomes the town or tribe hero, and the killing of a leopard starts a community celebration. The hunter keeps the skin, which is readily salable at prices ranging from five to forty American dollars, and the neighbors or the hunter and his family usually eat the meat, though in some tribes leopard meat is taboo. The leopard's teeth and claws make cherished presents. His skull is frequently used to adorn a wall or to store native medicine in. The successful leopard slayer expects and usually receives additional rewards in money or gifts. Among the Gbundis of Liberia the classic reward for killing a leopard is the donation of a wife by the chief, who as a rule has plenty to spare.

Cage traps baited with cassava roots or palm-kernel dough are used to catch hedgehogs and wild hogs. Schwab of Harvard's Peabody Museum staff told the following incident:

> "At Pandami [Liberia] a trapper had made a large fence [cage] trap and baited it with oil-palm nuts. . . . Four wild hogs entered, ate the bait, and went away because the trap had failed to spring and close the door. The trapper went home, washed his medicine to free it from evil, killed a fowl, daubed its blood over the medicine to feed and thus strengthen the medicine. . . . Then the trapper went back, rebaited and reset the trap, and that time the medicine worked. Twelve hogs were trapped.
>
> "With the help of a friend the hunter caught the biggest hog and set it free. Before allowing the hog to go the trapper stretched out his arms toward it and said: 'Go back to your people. Go tell them I am a good man. Go tell them all must come to my trap. I have all your brothers and children here.' "

One reason for the amount of trapping is that guns and ammunition are scarce, expensive, and usually, if available at all, antiquated. One still sees muzzle-loading flintlocks in use. These are loaded with black powder set off by flintlock sparks or percussion caps and they fire charges of iron scraps or chunks of surface iron ore. The charges are tamped with rags or wadded plant fiber. Wisely, the Liberian hunter usually fires his gun from his hip, not from his shoulder. And shotguns and shotgun shells are understandably the most coveted barter media of inland Liberia.

Slaying an elephant is the final and greatest deed of

hunting, a feat of superb courage and still greater skill. If the muzzle-loader is the only gun available, as is frequently the case, the powder charge must hurl out an oversize chisel or a homemade iron spear. High-powered cartridges fired from a suitable rifle simplify the feat, but—even so—elephant-slaying is never ping-pong. Immediately before the shortages of World War II stopped all supplies of heavy cartridges and rifles, as many as 300 elephants were reportedly slain in northern Liberia during a single year. Perhaps 150 would be near the present average for the nation's annual elephant bag.

Wild elephants, dangerous and destructive, are more numerous than before the war and the damage they do is greater. Because of this the Liberian Government has abandoned the costly license for elephant-hunting ($250 per year). And from the standpoint of the tribesmen the slaying of an elephant is a double blessing: it protects the rice crop and provides a vast amount of additional meat, since elephant is highly edible however tough.

The hunters go forth with prayer and strong medicines, and if the jungle gods are kindly and the hand artillery functions well, every vestige of the victim elephant can be chopped to pieces, dragged home, and eaten or somehow used. Usually the chief supervises the division of the spoils, taking as his own reward the tail (which in some places designates the chief's office) and at least one of the tusks. The elephant's feet are used to make bracelets, and the skull is a precious trophy. The elephant slayer is entitled to divide the bulk of the carcass among his friends, relatives, or townsmen, having saved out all the meat he and his immediate family can use. He also holds the honor place at the celebration and receives esteem and suitable rewards perhaps including an extra wife.

Elephant-hunting is the most heroic brand of Liberian sport. But there are various more modest ones, such as the game drive wherein a number of hunters, sometimes the entire able-bodied male population of a village, set up nets at strategic locations, and fan out and walk through the forest, beating the bushes and waving tree branches to flush small game. In a bolder mood, huntsmen sometimes go out in pairs, and in the deep bush imitate the cries of wounded antelope or other bush animals to attract roving leopards and other killers. But team hunting, even at best, is dangerous.

The jungle hunter must be skilled and brave, his work being as dangerous as it is useful. By tribe tradition the hunter must maintain high standards of personal honor in keeping with his great calling. It is a vital social and economic symbol; for what the hunter is primarily doing is to meet a need: trapping and killing meat, that protein food so crucially required for the health and survival of his people. This vital need for hunting and trapping is to be duplicated in few other areas of the contemporary world. In Liberia the lack of meat and other protein foods is the greatest threat to health and progress. The fertile soil might become pastures and ranges for domesticated meat stock, but the jungle bush continues to crowd away the grasses that would support meat animals. And until great progress is made in the planned raising of livestock and in transportation, Liberia would face disaster if the amount of wild-animal life were to be seriously reduced. For some time to come the country must get most of its meat from the jungle.

Chapter Four

From the Tribes

Africa is the linguist's hunting ground. The continent has some eight hundred indigenous languages, and in Liberia alone one can hear at least forty of them. The official tongue is English: a distinctive, always interesting composite of English as spoken in the High Street and in Harvard Square, on Broadway and on Basin Street.

But like her African neighbors, Liberia keeps many of her tribal languages alive and in use. As a rule the Monrovian and many other Liberians speak fluent English without any trace of the synthetic "darky" talk which most certainly is not and never was real Negro talk. Many also speak several of the native Liberian languages, such as Mano, Bussie, or Kpessi, and not infrequently French, Spanish, Portuguese, or German, usually learned in the course of attending European or British schools. In general, Liberia's English is considerably like the language of contemporary England, though conspicuously less "British" than the speech common in British African colonies, which tends strongly toward the "Oxfordian." Liberian English retains much of the structural rhythm and distinctive vitality of true African talk.

Beyond the corporate limits of Monrovia, and occasionally within them, one becomes acquainted with the strange phenomenon called "pidgin English," which keeps straying farther from the work jargon that Portuguese and other roving traders presumably coined and introduced so widely.

Many of the basic pidgin English words are not English at all, but are adaptations: "savvy" from the Spanish *sabe* (to understand), "palaver" from the Portuguese *palavra* (to make talk), and so on. In rural Liberia you learn, for example, that the verb "to be" is the pivot of pidgin. But the adapted pidgin or "bush talk" of backcountry Liberia dispenses with all past and future tenses of "to be," using only the present tense. The tribe-member uses "I be, you be, they be, or he be," yet oddly enough avoids "it be" or "she be" since the bush talk has neither feminine nor neuter gender. He usually makes his future tenses with the help of "go" and his past tenses with the help of "been." When he says "I go make," he means that he "will go in the more or less immediate future." When he says "I been go," he means that he has already gone. "Live," is more or less synonymous with "to be." One may thus hear such curious sentences as this: "This woman, he live small for die"—meaning "This woman is almost dead."

As a rule, "for" is used instead of "to"—e.g., "I go for Monrovia." But, strangely, "for" can also mean "in" or "on." There is no use for our common pronoun "us," or for "ours" or any other possessive. In pidgin the possessive is established by the use of "to" or "for." "It is ours" becomes "He be for we" or "He be we part." The word "part" also indicates the possessive. "Our house" becomes "we part house." The word "pass" indicates the comparative. "From here go Kakata be far more pass from here go Monrovia" merely means "Kakata is farther from here than Monrovia." Confusingly, however, "pass" can and frequently does mean "not understandable." "Englishman he pass me" means "I simply cannot understand Englishmen."

If you were to say to a jungle man "Let go!" meaning "Leave it alone!" he would most probably grasp the object in question and go hiking away with the greatest possible speed. In pidgin "let go" is "leave it," pronounced "lef it." "Let go" would be understood as meaning "let's go," which is one of the few phrases in pidgin that mean what they say.

"Lock," in pidgin, means to close, to fasten, or to heal. One locks one's mouth or the window or the water spigot. A wound locks itself when it heals. In pidgin all meat is beef. Call for fine beef and you may find yourself eating monkey meat, elephant meat, chicken, or pork, or a combination thereof. Recently a traveler while driving inland from Monrovia saw a group of about twelve native road workers happily barbecuing a fieldmouse which of them had caught. "Small beef, boss!" one of the workmen explained.

In pidgin, "meat" is literally a live animal—which usually means a wild animal since there are extremely few domestic animals. "Find" means to look for, and "look" means "see" or "find." So the question: "Did you find it, Johnny?" is likely to bring the answer: "Yes, I find him all side but I no look him," meaning "No, I've looked for it everywhere but I can't find it." "Just now" can mean either the near future or the near past. "Soon time" means either "by and by" or the comparatively distant future. The faraway past is "first time." "Now, now!" means "this instant." "One time" means "right away." "One, one" means a few; and "one" frequently means "alone." "Merry Christmas" is "Happy Dashes" (gifts).

Pidgin or bush-talk phrases creep into moderately correct English like weeds into a poorly tended garden. With obviously good cause, Liberians through their schools, their missions, and their government offices seek to thwart the encroachments of pidgin into their resources in legitimate English. But the indigenous and bona-fide languages of

Liberia still serve the people and therefore are to be respected both for their utility and for their history. Liberia has, for example, the distinguished tribal language called Kpelle, or Kpwessi, one of the dozens of so-called Bantu languages that are spoken throughout Equatorial Africa. Almost every Bantu language has a number of local dialects. The tribe languages of the Liberian Bussies and Gbandis are very similar to Kpwessi; so much so that the respective tribesmen can understand each other after a very few days' acquaintance.

Bantu languages are "tonal"; that is, the same word has several distinct meanings depending on whether it is spoken in a high, a medium, or a low pitch. There may be and frequently are as many as five different tones, and therefore five different meanings, for the same word; and tonal qualities of indigenous languages are frequently discernible in Liberian pronunciations of English. The Bantu vocabularies are made up of nouns, verbs, and pronouns. There are no articles or prepositions, extremely few adjectives or adverbs, and no distinct genders. This too has influenced the prevailing Liberian use of English. In Kpwessi, the four common tonal distinctions are the high, the low, the rising, and the falling. Tonal implications are stronger for verbs than for nouns. For example, depending on its tone qualities, *"kapa"* means "you came," "you have come," "you may come," or "you must come."

One presently learns that in most Bantu languages there are three groups or classes of nouns, each with a definite and an indefinite form. To establish the definite form one changes the first letter of the indefinite form and adds an "i" to the end of the word. Thus in Kpwessi, *wulu* means "any tree"; *ngului* means "this particular tree." *Ta* is *a* town; *dai* is *the* town. In shaping sentences the object of the transitive verb is placed immediately before the verb. Thus when a Kpwessi says "The woman saw a leopard," he is really saying "The woman she a leopard saw." In place of saying "The man is tall," he says "The man has length"—substituting a noun of quality for the nonexistent adjective. You hear of "a running," "a playing," "an eating," "a sleeping," "a killing," "a growing," etc. Numbering is based on fives instead of tens; you count one, two, three, four, five, five-on-one, five-on-two, five-on-three.

I am not writing a thesis on Liberian-African languages. But, as any reporter learns even before going upcountry from Monrovia, the indigenous languages are important in inland Liberia, the great reservoir of the Negro tribes. To understand and to appreciate Liberia as a contemporary republic, some attention must be given to the inland tribes.

The tribal society is pivotal, and the tribe is at the same time an agrarian commune, a fraternal association, and a confederation of families, a colonizing institution, a lingual group, a protective group, a congregation, and a government. Tribe villages, with populations ranging from a dozen or less to more than a thousand, become merged into clan groups, frequently of four to six thousand. As a rule, two or more clans compose the tribe.

The tribes are distinctive, even in terms of anthropology. Some are made up principally of tall and rather stately people; others are preponderantly squat and fat. Some are almost ebony black; others are brown-skinned. Some of the tribes are Moslem; others have taken Christianity seriously; still more have kept to tribe rituals of worship, pantheistic or pagan. In some tribes the manual crafts are stressed. Some are almost wholly agricultural. Some are mainly traders and others boatmen. For example, the far-scattered Krus are the great waterfront people of Liberia and much of West Africa. Such tribes as the Gbundes and Lomas are the mountaineers of Liberia. More populous tribes, such as the Mano, Gio, and Ge, are the lowland or hillside people.

Each tribe cherishes its own particular folk lore, history, and tradition and, with few or no exceptions, each tribe has its own story of creation. The "singer" for a paramount chief of the Gio recites the genesis of that tribe as follows:

> "The first father of all people is Ye. There was a woman, too, also named Ye. They were twins. They had a son named Abi. He in turn had one son named Za. Za had much power to bring good or evil upon people. He is petitioned . . . even yet, thus: *Za, bo kende* [help me]. If one wants anything very much he makes this petition.
>
> "Abi caught one of each animal of the town. If he had caught animals of the forest they would have run away again. The town animals he caught were goat, dog, cow, sheep, cat and chicken. He said: 'I don't want my son to be without a wife.' Then he took his medicine and blew some of it on each of the animals. This turned them into six maidens. . . . Abi said: 'You, cat-woman, you are my son's wife because you stay around the house all day. If I gave him the dog-woman she would follow other men continually. The cow-woman you would have to drive behind the others.'
>
> "The cat-woman was a peacemaker. She is the mother of peacemakers because she remains quiet and peaceful around the house. The cat does not like a palaver or quarrels in the house. That is why she carries out her kittens and hides them when there is trouble in the house. The cat that was turned to a woman bore Za two sons, Sera and Zuakpwa, twins. To these Za gave all the other animal women. The cat-woman was his own. Her last son was Ma. To him Za turned over all his household because Ma was a wise man. He was the father of the Ma-Me [Mano] and the Ge-Ne [Gio]. That is why these really great tribes are wiser than Za's other descendants."

Here is d'Ollone's translation of the genesis of the Graoros clan of the Grebo tribe of southeast Liberia:

> "One day the people were assembled to celebrate the death of an elephant. While they were eating this good game an old and unknown woman came, wishing to partake of the feast. Everyone drove her away except one man named Ouro. He gave her a piece of meat.
>
> "At nightfall she pulled him aside and told him that she was the head of that country. He was to assemble his household and flee immediately. . . . They went across the Cavally River and became the founders of the Graoro clan. Immediately after they left, a rain of stones fell on Nienokoue, burying all its inhabitants. These heaped-up rocks form the mountain called Nienokoue."

There are at least as many folk stories of creation as there are tribes. I recall the one about Nipala and his wife Titi who left their home on the far side of the Cavally River. When they came to the banks of the muddy river they found it in high flood. As they stood there with no way of crossing the flood a leopard happened along and took them on his back. That is why Nipala's tribe does not eat leopard.

And there are remarkable legends about magic robes, singing waters, and petrified villages. "The people who were turned to stone can be seen doing just what they were engaged in at the time. There are two men, one whispering into the ear of the other; a woman looking for vermin on the head of another woman; a pregnant woman sitting down; and a woman grinding rice – all turned to stones."

The significance and the historical importance of the Liberian tribes are still inadequately known. In a general way we know that the tribes of inland Liberia and a great deal of Africa have grown from the merging of families and clans, or groups of families. The Mano, for example, one of the largest of Liberian tribes, is a tribal federation of the clans of the Bei, Ga, Yamei, Kei, Gbana, Beua, Duro, Gbwai, Gbwen, Kpibe, Lau, Yalur, Yeka, Za, and Zo.

The birth and growth of clans and tribes appears to proceed more or less as follows: In the beginning a man took a wife (or several wives), moved into a favored part of the jungle, and began a family. As the family increased and as the jungle yielded more abundantly, the family head bought, captured, or otherwise acquired additional wives from other families or clans. In time and with due process of propagation the larger families grew into clans. They built villages for themselves, added fields, and chose their patriarchs or stronger men as village chiefs. In time the strongest or the best-liked of the village chiefs were elevated to clan chiefs. As towns and clans increased, they tended to become merged into nations or tribes, each one led by a supreme or paramount chief.

Anthropologists seem inclined to agree that the earlier peoples of Liberia, like those of Equatorial Africa as a whole, sprang from small farming villages scattered throughout the vast rain forests. Mutual protection was probably the first incentive for federation. Time and again the stronger tribes or bands swept over the unprotected or less protected villages, killing or enslaving the men and carrying away the women and children. Frequently, too, pestilences or famines left isolated villages incapable of self-defense. A Loma tribesman of Liberia tells a typical clan story: "Our fathers lived in hamlets of three or four huts each. Too many wars drove the people farther and farther back into the high bush. Many were taken captives. Many were slain by the marauders. So those who lived came together and drank medicine on which they had sworn they would live together in big towns and be brothers there . . . quit fighting among themselves and protect each other. That is why we of the Loma have big towns."

The early jungle settlements grew into agricultural communes. By comparison with American or European towns, not many of the tribal communities are big. In backcountry Liberia the majority of native towns have from thirty to ninety huts, or "roofs," with an average of six or seven people to each hut. Frequently the smaller hamlets, usually farm suburbs of the towns, have only two or three or at most a dozen huts and are commonly called half-towns. Tribal towns with from 150 to 200 huts are impressively big; those with 600, 800, or even 1200 huts are jungle cities.

Quite logically the larger towns and the more populous tribes tended to gravitate toward the more fertile valleys or to the river banks. Many ghost towns or dying hamlets may still be seen along the old trade roads and trails that during dark and bloody centuries carried the tragic processions of slaves captured in farther inland valleys and marched under whip and shackles to seacoast stockades and slave ships. There is reason to believe that hundreds of inland villages were completely depopulated by the slave trade, while thousands more were robbed of a large part of their population. Accordingly, for self-preservation, many of the tribespeople moved their towns and villages away from the roads and trails far back into inaccessible forest lands and hills.

More recently a great many tribal towns have been moved to hidden clearings in incredibly dense jungles because of the need for conserving food. African etiquette demands the granting of food and shelter to the traveler. All villages that are located beside trade routes or through roads or trails face having to supply free food and shelter to the hundreds or thousands of passersby. Many a generous chief has been made poor and in time deposed as a result of yielding to the noble African mandate of hospitality, and many a village, otherwise prosperous, has been abandoned when its citizens found themselves unable to provide the wherewithal of African etiquette and still contrive to save a few grains of rice for themselves.

For various other good reasons, villages die and others are born. Not infrequently the water supply fails. Sometimes, for reasons not easy to explain, the game and the fruit vanish from near-by jungle lands or forests. Occasionally, too, during the dry seasons, villages are destroyed by fire. Other tribal towns have died as their soil became exhausted and their people were obliged to move to new farm sites and to clear new fields. Still others have been decimated by epidemics or contagious diseases. Many have vanished when the boundaries of clan or tribal territories were changed as a result of chiefs' palaver. Repeatedly new towns are born when clans permit strangers to join them and take over new fields and build new huts.

Though some of the tribes are ancient, extremely few of the hut villages or towns are more than a quarter-century or at most a half-century old. Only occasionally one finds convincing evidence of great age in a settlement. As one exceptional instance, there is a Buzzi town in the north or Mano country of Liberia where the market place has become several feet lower than the adjoining land presumably as a result of having been swept so often. But in the main the marks of time disappear quickly. Lusty bush soon blots out the rice fields or cotton patches, or the lime or orange trees of other years. Even the roadside shrines — medicine huts built beside the trail as insurance against sickness and wild animals — are quickly crowded into dank oblivion by the invincible, deathless vegetation. Sacred trees, such as the wild teak which is frequently used to mark the graves of departed chiefs, presently become lost in second growth. All in all, it is advisable to look closely at today's villages – they may be somewhere else tomorrow.

It is astonishing how unexpectedly you can come upon jungle towns. You may be tramping along, thinking of nothing in particular, when the trail turns – and there you are in another village. It may be the great town of a clan chief with as many as 5,000 tribesmen. It is more likely to be a mere shady spot, a half-town, with three or four conical huts. The chances are that you will be a great deal more surprised by seeing the town than the town is by seeing you. Usually the coming of a stranger is announced far in advance of the actual arrival by the voices of signal drums or the unexplainable faculties of grapevine telepathy. In any case unseen eyes are watching.

It is always possible to stumble into a tribe village much as you would stumble into an open ditch. The bush trails are not always easy to follow. In the backcountry one finds occasional strips of cleared roadways entirely unconnected with any other roads. Sometimes the trails between friendly villages are kept open as a symbol of tribal amity, but if friendship between neighbors has cooled, the trails are permitted to grow up in bush so dense that only an expert can locate the trail site. Thus it is sometimes easier to happen upon a tribe village than to find it deliberately.

In place of the American post office or court house, the functional center of the tribal village is the palaver house. The chief and his elders convene at the palaver house almost daily and the tribesmen come to discuss and settle their numerous problems, differences, and claims. Frequently, too, the palaver house serves double use as the trophy house or village museum. Often it is the village medicine house and, at recurring intervals, the headquarters for dancing and rituals. Usually it is the biggest building in the town: an oversize hut, round with walls built of packed mud and a conical roof made of native thatch. In some villages it is rectangular with a steeply sloping thatched roof and open sides that are sheltered from the sun and blowing rain by curtains made of raffia palm.

Whatever its architecture, the palaver hut is the landmark of the town. As a rule it is tidy and clean, which in general is true of the village as a whole. Unlike the fields and forests that surround them, the country villages are rarely green. Sometimes they are dotted with common African flowers such as the red canna or the big blue or pink hibiscus. The outskirts may be marked by stubby citrus trees that bear rough, green-skinned oranges with extremely sweet juice, or huge, bright green lemons that are extremely sour. There may be ragged rows of native sugar cane, lines of banana plants, or oil palms bowed with heavy clusters of kernels. Sometimes the lanes are shaded with vividly green avocado trees whose branches sag with rich green or purple-skinned butter pears.

Certain country villages, however, are entirely barren of vegetation. Their narrow streets are swept clean and the rain and sunlight fall impartially on the rows of round mud huts topped with thatched roofs shaped like inverted ice-cream cones. Town life is an unending round of housecleaning, street-sweeping, laundering, and bathing. Filth or untidiness is deemed disgraceful. A good chief never permits grass to grow in the street of his town, and he demands the utmost cleanliness of his people.

The jungle frontier of Liberia today is in a sense very like the American frontier of a century ago. The basic pattern endures, with an ingeniously simple subsistence agriculture the mainstay of the land and the people.

The dry season, which usually begins in November and continues to May, is the principal farming season, the time when the great majority of able-bodied tribesmen – men, women, and children alike – turn farmers. During the heavy rainy season, which stretches over most of the rest of the year, some men hunt and trade, while others more adventurous, tramp away to work in mines or plantations, with the chief's permission and after promising to return home in time to help plant the next year's crops.

Meanwhile the home-stayers wait and listen at the palaver house, and gossip and visit at the tribal smithy – the men's particular refuge. The women keep house, crack the oil kernels, rise early to beat and winnow the rice, and cook the food for their menfolk and children. They walk in file to the near-by creeks or rivers, fill water jugs, balance the jugs on their heads, and so provide their husbands' daily hot bath. They tend their babies and young children. On rainy days they occupy themselves with combing and spinning fibers for cloth, and making fish nets, and keeping watch on family holdings of chickens, goats, or sheep, and making brief journeys in quest of peppers, palm and cola nuts, or wild fruits. They carry produce to the local markets and there buy, sell, trade, barter, and gossip.

Life in the tribal towns holds to a constant pattern. Old people sit about and talk of long ago. Naked babies, ornamentally smeared with white clay, roll, scoot, and toddle in doorways. Young men carve and pound out implements for the forthcoming farming season, or brew and drink palm wine. Hunters boast of their quarry and fishermen describe their catches. Children frolic in the village street, pounding drums or gasoline tins, stamping out energetic rhythms with their bare feet, improvising singing games and rain games and carefree versions of others that mark childhood anywhere in the world.

At work the tribesman usually plods or at least moves deliberately. But at play his spontaneity, his capacity for laughter and mimicry and pantomime, spring up in high-spirited magic. In the blink of an eye a solemn processional changes to a hilariously funny burlesque in which the players suddenly assume the roles of jaunty British "clarks," or pompous district commissioners, or one-stop, one-time "African experts" from abroad.

The tribal life holds infinite variety. It is both traditional and spontaneous, dignified and slapstick, planned and extemporaneous. And it is a life for the night as well as for the day. The night is the time for dancing – for group dances and solo dances that tell stories few white men, if any, can comprehend. It is the time for songs and drums and the amazing world of drums. There are giant drums that serve as fire sirens or alarms. There are big war drums made of huge logs with one end hollowed, then covered over with taut skins, and sometimes raised eight or ten feet above the ground so that the drummer must stand on a high platform in order to reach the head. These war drums roar and boom. The dancing drums are made of home-cured parchment stretched over hollowed wood; these are frequently set in groups, with one drummer or "singer" beating lustily on four or five different drums.

There are also double-headed drums, generally similar to snare drums and beaten with the fingers and the heels of the hands. The smaller "talking drums" are sometimes shaped like hour-glasses; they are carried under the singer's left arm and beaten with a stick, as accompaniment for bigger drums, or as inspiration for the women working in the field or preparing a meal. Other smaller drums are fashioned of slit bamboo. A single block of hardwood is used for the big kettledrum; a balance brace or "foot" protrudes from the bottom, and the head is ringed with bands of iron or brass to vary the pitch and give the instrument a "tinkle."

I am told by Liberian tribesmen that at least in some towns every man has his own drum name or "call," and that drum telegraphy is so well coded that other tribespeople – even those who live a long way off and speak a different language – can send and receive word of a stranger's arrival or the coming of soldiers, of invitations to feasts or dances, of wrestling bouts, of planting or harvest bees, or of any other headline news of the countryside.

The songs and the talk of the drums are supplemented by other native instruments such as primitive banjos and cymbals, bells and rattles, whistles made of pottery or crab-claws, bamboo flutes, animal horns, squawkers, trumpets made of elephant tusks, and so on.

If dancing and music-making are the supreme recreations, juggling and wrestling are the favorite sports; and for both of these there are village and tribal champions. Sometimes the jugglers toss and catch young children instead of balls or chunks of wood. The tribal wrestlers are often remarkably skilful, far more so than those who wallow and puff on padded mats here in the United States. Backcountry wrestling is distinctly formal. Contestants begin by "measuring for size," face each other and grip hands, release hands and slap thighs, then open the bout. Apparently no holds are barred, but (so mission doctors have told me) tribal wrestlers are rarely hurt in combat. In some of the tribes women also wrestle, and win and hold championships. Regardless of sex, the winners are duly acclaimed and rewarded. Girls crowd about the man champion, pat his chest, and heap him with praises.

Style and apparel are likewise parts of the tribal life. In general, the men appear to be more dress-conscious than the women. Particularly in the more remote areas, chiefs and other important men freqeuntly wear "bubus"—homespun blankets with head holes in the center and striped lengthwise. For this stately dress the cloth is often of handsome quality, and both fabrics and colors are chosen with outstanding artistic skill.

The tribesmen's usual dress is a sort of improvised toga, wrapped sarong-style about the waist and draped upward and over the left shoulder. In the jungle country shoes are rarely worn except by chiefs, though leather or cloth sandals are frequently worn by non-tribe members. Headwear is various: hats, red fezzes, cylindrical caps of homespun cloth, ornamented head pads or skull caps, brimmed hats of home-woven raffia fiber, or adaptations of hats common in the United States and Europe. For work garb and for boys' wear, the singlet or unattached upper section of men's underwear has come into widespread fashion. Since in prewar days most of the singlets were made in Japan, World War II produced a dire shortage, and as this book is written they are still in short supply.

Though the women's clothing is usually less costly than the men's, it is more varied and ingenious. Their apparel does not consist of "dresses" in the usual sense of the word; rather it consists of inventive windings and drapings of the fabric which are interestingly and conveniently adaptable. I confess to a real, if naive and amateurish, admiration for these clothes, particularly for the instinctive grace with which they are worn and the talent for improvisation that they show. I have seen gowns and wrap-arounds made of brightly patterned batiks and other imported bolt cloths, their colors gay and tasteful, frequently chic and brilliant. Country cloth is commoner, however — home-woven cotton, usually dark blue but sometimes white ornamented with circles woven in narrow strips and casually sewed together. I am told that the beaded girdle is a staple accessory; I myself never saw any.

For work clothing the women usually wear the abbreviated leaf-skirt, though this is often supplemented in unexpected ways: an apron made of skin, a brightly colored turban, loose-fitting skin sandals — though normally the women go barefoot. You will see them tramping by wearing only the leaf-skirt but carrying, neatly packed in their *kinjas* or head baskets, their town or "palaver" clothes.

I have mentioned the turbans, but this is only one of the many types of headcovering to be seen. There are brimmed hats woven of rattan strips; umbrella-shaped hats; tufted hats made of skins. The "trimmings" may be feathers or plumes, berries or dwarf yellow bananas or undersized oranges. It occasionally struck me that the New York milliners must long have been pirating Liberian styles! If not, they are missing a trick and should travel to West Africa for models, since — to me, at least, a mere man — the feminine headgear there is irresistibly fetching.

And the same holds for "costume jewelry." The womenfolk of some of the tribes, particularly Gio, glitter and tinkle with necklaces and rings and miscellaneous jewelry, made usually of iron, bronze, or brass. But you will also see necklaces of silver and beads of multicolored clay. There are anklets of silver, too, and strings of leopard and chimpanzee teeth, and leg-bands of aluminum and iron and other metals.

As a rule, the women are passionately fond of perfumes, of necessity homemade perfumes, and one is continually aware that with almost no exceptions the tribespeople are clean. Daily or twice-daily baths are a classic practice of most Liberians and other West Africans. Also they cleanse their teeth, usually with softwood twigs. They are always eager to buy soap and diligent in making their own out of palm oil and wood ashes. Children and women frequently rub their faces and bodies with fine white clay, just as their forebears did centuries before the day of the billion-dollar mass industry of cosmetics.

Many of the tribeswomen are handsome, some distinctly beautiful. Those belonging to certain tribes are preponderantly short and plump; but most are outstandingly graceful and erect, moving, standing, and working with dignity.

The jungle ways are unfathomably old, yet in some respects they are impressively new. The facts given thus far in this chapter are at least generally true of tribal Liberia today. But inevitably the jungle land, like all others, changes. Roads reach farther into the remote hills and valleys, and along these roads traders, merchandise, and a changing world follow. But the tribe represents more than a group of people and a chief: it means group work, group play, community housing, and defense. The tribe is the basis of the social establishment. Frequently all the members — men, women, and children alike — are obliged to work for their community without pay. They clear lands and build roads for the common good of the tribe. With the chief's permission or by his order, the men leave their homes, take employment beyond tribal boundaries, and then at the chief's discretion return. These men are duty bound to bring back at least part of their earnings, either in money or (preferably) in useful goods.

In return for work and services, each tribe member is entitled to a measure of social security. When he is old and unable to earn, the tribe is obliged to support him. And a good tribesman is expected to help his neighbors during times of hunger or other visitations of distress. Unfortunately the tribes' care of the sick is still far short of what is needed; too often the extremely sick are relegated to improvised isolation during their final illness. The tribe as a whole must take care of its orphans and its aged or hungering members. It is therefore easy to understand why the tribal African profoundly pities his American brothers who were carried off to slavery and thereby robbed of all the heritages and advantages of the tribe.

Inherently the tribe's obligations are those of any sovereign government in the world today. From certain points of view the Republic of Liberia is actually a federation of tribes, all tribe members being admitted to citizenship. As equity owners of tribe lands and other tribe properties, all tribespeople, men and women alike, are qualified to vote and take part in the national government – which, as in any national government, heightens the citizens' responsibilities and makes for greater federal strength.

One of the obligations of each tribe and clan, admitted through its chief, is the payment of taxes. During earlier times, when currency was scarce or nonexistent, taxes were paid in rice or in manual labor; but most interior taxes are now paid in United States money. The basic tribal tax (in some instances the only one) is the annual hut tax, at present two dollars per hut, an average of about forty cents per capita for the tribe membership.

Other tax levies – as severance, excise, or income taxes – rarely affect the tribesmen. The Frontier Police Force, commanded by the President, is maintained to supervise law enforcement and tax collections in the hinterland. At various times in the past the Frontier Force has been accused of usurping the authority of chiefs and of conduct detrimental to tribe welfare. Fortunately, the number and the seriousness of these charges have diminished during recent years. But it has been thoroughly proved that when the military collects excessive taxes, steals or destroys livestock or other tribe properties, subjects chiefs to indignities, persecutes certain tribes, or causes them to be deprived of needed lands, the consequences imperil not only the immediate victims, but in a very real sense the entire nation.

Any serious impairment of a tribe's political or economic integrity is almost invariably synonymous with infinite suffering and adversity. Excessive taxation quickly destroys the incentive for growing crops and marketing surpluses, substantiating the tribesman's position that "if Government be bound to take it we not grow it." That attitude (by no means limited to Liberia) poses an essential issue on which depends the Republic's survival. For the most part the current Tubman administration, while paying the national debt, has insisted that tax levies on the tribes be proportional to the proved earning power of the tribal citizenship.

In particular the Liberian Government now seeks the coöperation of the tribes in building roads as a means of releasing manpower, stabilizing prices, and augmenting the flow of trade into the interior. When rice and other products of the tribes cannot be carried to market, there is no real incentive for increasing acreages and thus protecting a region from famine. Moreover, when essentials such as salt must be carried into the interior on the heads of tribesmen, the same pack of salt may be worth ten cents a pound at point A and a dollar a pound at point B a mere hundred miles upcountry. The issue of roads versus foot trails, of trucks versus head loads, grows ever more important to the tribe and the nation alike. A strong carrier on a fairly smooth trail can walk about fifteen miles per day; a sturdy truck can average at least ten times that distance even on a frontier road. One five-ton truck can do the work of at least five hundred head carriers – provided, of course, that the truck has roads on which to travel. Obviously Liberia needs trucks and roads. She also needs the tribes.

The coördination and integration of the tribe with a republican government is gradually achieving success. This constitutes a big story that we shall presently view in greater detail.

Chapter Five

Liberia and Rubber

PART OF the deep tropics, Liberia is a veritable paradise for trees. Her soil is fertile and the greater part of her land is suitable for growing most of the staple tropical crops in world trade, and a number of temperate-zone crops as well. But trees come first, and tree crops, such as natural rubber, possess inherent advantages.

Liberia has always been an agricultural nation and at no time during the past century has there been any doubt that her fortunes would be largely determined by crops for export. In 1910, her most critical year, the place of Liberian crops in world trade was still extremely uncertain. The earlier exports remained: palm oils and fibers, coffee, wild rubber, other tree crops of the jungle edge, and the occasional cargo of gold, ivory, or skins. But many other tropical lands – for the most part colonies of strongly industrialized empires – were producing much longer lists of tropical staples in much greater quantities and at lower costs.

The year 1910 was a memorable year in tropical history as a whole. That part of the world lying between latitudes 20 degrees north and 20 degrees south was changing to meet the demands of industrial economics, and for the first time rubber began to replace spices as the preëminent export from the hot lands. Liberian soils and forest sites were as plainly suited to growing rubber trees as those of many another bigger, more populous, and less isolated tropical country. But Liberia was still poor, and by 1910 it was evident that tropical exports were unavoidably influenced or dominated by international bargaining and politics. Agricultural economics were made at treaty tables, or at corporation board meetings, as well as in warm rich earth.

As the automotive age took form the rubber tire was becoming the symbol of a new economic epoch. But the tropical world moves at its own tempo, and Liberia continued its struggle for national survival with minimum relations with the outside world, and without autos, roads, or railroads. The Liberian forests then could offer no more of the great new crop of the tropics than the tiny yields of the lobelia vine and such unimpressive latex-bearing trees as *Ficus elastica.*

The story of Liberian exports and living standards remained sad and bleak. The Republic's annual revenue was often less than $300,000, sometimes as low as $125,000 – sums that simply were not enough. Though times were hard in all West Africa, they were exceptionally so in Liberia, becoming even worse as the oncoming shadow of World War I was replaced by the reality. As the European war spread, Britain was obliged to make drastic reductions in her merchant shipping along the West African coast, which resulted in an abrupt halving of Liberia's revenue from custom duties. Since practically four-fifths of the Liberian government's income had been derived from this source, the resulting body blow to her economy was little short of disastrous.

When in 1918 Liberia joined the Allies, it seemed as though the situation might improve. Great Britain agreed to lighten the shipping restrictions provided Liberia would deport all her German nationals. Liberia agreed: the Germans were deported aboard a French cruiser – but Britain did not supply the promised shipping. At that time American loans were being poured forth freely, and Woodrow

Wilson promised $5,000,000 to Liberia – but the loan never materialized. Instead, a group of American bankers – including J. P. Morgan & Company, Kuhn, Loeb & Company, and the National City and First National Banks of New York, "acting for themselves and for others" – advanced a routine credit loan. This required the Liberian government, while repaying the loan and interest, to employ and pay an American financial commissioner and twenty-two other American employees – at an annual cost of $109,700, or about one-fifth of Liberia's entire annual expenditures.

World War I plainly stressed the country's need of investment capital. Repeatedly from Monrovia came legislative resolutions and presidential communiqués making it plain that Liberia desired and needed bona fide development enterprises – constructive works to develop and expand her evident though still little realized resources – and that Liberians preferred earning to borrowing.

Hopefully Liberia joined the League of Nations. Though the Congress of the United States declined to grant the $5,000,000 loan which President Wilson had specifically promised as a "moral mandate," Liberia continued retiring a total of $1,200,000 in bonds held by foreign banks and investors. This called for dime-counting and severe sacrifices. The scarcity of ships continued to reduce customs collections. Intermittently the Liberian bonds sagged, and the Government's credit dipped, until by 1924 it found itself unable to raise a mere $25,000 from the sale of national bonds. Nevertheless, Liberia continued to live and to pay . . . and to feel more clearly than ever the trends and pulses of a shrinking world.

Far beyond the severely reduced boundaries of Liberia, and beyond the immediate range of her interests, one of the most important industrial trends of the times was taking shape. The industry of natural rubber had become world-wide in an unprecedented merging and welding of theory, social philosophy, complex chemistry, industrial craftsmanship, international economy, and hard-driving exploitation.

The decade between 1904 and 1914 established natural rubber as a hugely and increasingly important international crop of the tropics. It proved that the graceful, dappled-bark Hevea tree *(Hevea brasiliensis)* of upper South America was the best provider of natural rubber. In the same decade this Amazon Basin jungle tree was lifted out of the all-too-trusting hands of South Americans and established as the basis of a formidable crop cartel in British Malaya, the Netherlands Indies, Ceylon, and other populous and temporarily docile hot lands.

By the close of World War I, at least 97 percent of all rubber in use was coming from Hevea trees, and rubber was rapidly pushing ahead of coffee, sugar cane, fibers, and palm oils as the most valuable and strategic tropical crop in international trade. And rubber production was changing from a difficult, oftentimes perilous snatch-grab from tropical wilds to an effective merging of plantation agronomy and highly productive forestry. The productive value of the tens of millions of wild Hevea trees of the Amazon Basin was rapidly vanishing, while in the hot coolie lands below and beyond Singapore new rubber plantations were supplying most of the material for a growing industry. British- and European-controlled plantation companies were developing the most audacious and profitable crop monopoly of the twentieth century.

Factories in the United States were actually making about three-fourths of all the rubber goods used by mankind, and the United States public alone was consuming more than half of all rubber manufactures. As the automotive age continued to flourish and increase, United States imports of rubber had climbed from a few thousand tons to hundreds of thousands of tons yearly. Yet from a standpoint of natural rubber supply, the Far East planters — preponderantly British and Dutch, with a minor fringe of French — held all the trump cards in the rubber deck.

When the time came they played these cards with a vengeance. During the depression of 1920-21, rubber along with other commodities slumped in price. At that time the British controlled about 75 percent of the rubber-producing areas in the East. The British growers concocted a plan for restricting production of rubber, known as the "Stevenson Scheme" or Stevenson Rubber Restriction Act. Becoming effective in November 1922, it provided that no rubber could be exported without a license. A board was created to determine what production would be allowed in quotas on a quarterly basis to maintain a "reasonable price."

When the act went into effect rubber was selling around 14 cents a pound. The growers claimed that all they wanted to accomplish by the Government decree was to increase the price to about 36 cents, which as everybody knew would give them an excellent profit. But the legislation provided no ceiling, and by 1925 rubber had soared to $1.23 a pound.

With the quick, enormous profits that came with this monopoly also came retribution. The Dutch Government refused to join the restriction plan. During the life of the Stevenson plan rubber growers of the Netherlands Indies had all the advantages of price control without the limitations on production. As a result, when the Stevenson scheme was finally abandoned in 1928, the Dutch had increased their production from around 25 percent of the rubber grown in the Pacific East to about 48 percent, while the British exportation had decreased proportionately.

But during the six-year life of restriction American consumers of rubber wares paid at least one and a quarter billion dollars as direct bounties to the rubber cartel. On the whole, American rubber manufacturers had docilely accepted the conditions of the Stevenson scheme as a matter of course, and most of them assumed to see no reason for getting excited about the restriction act, although it was plain that it would cost the helpless American consumers hundreds of millions of dollars a year.

However, this was not the position of one prominent American industrialist, who for some time had been concerned over tire-rubber monopoly. When word came of the enactment of the Stevenson plan, he courageously and lone-handedly swung into vigorous action. This was the pioneer rubber manufacturer, Harvey S. Firestone, who had founded the Firestone Tire & Rubber Company and built it into a worldwide organization. He had had plenty of experience in fighting cartels, as the history of his struggle against patent monopolies had shown.

Firestone had long been convinced that Americans should produce their own rubber, this in order to assure dependable and adequate supplies of a vital material in case of a national emergency and to safeguard American consumers from the clearly demonstrated incompetencies and tyrannies of alien rubber cartels. Firestone factories required rubber in ever-increasing quantities. But their founder's conviction that rubber should be produced, bought, sold, and distributed on a free, competitive market represented more than the business judgment of one manufacturer – it was also a moral conviction.

As an industrial statesman, Harvey S. Firestone elected to spearhead – under the banner "Americans Should Produce Their Own Rubber" – what he deemed an essential American crusade, and he was not deterred by the fact that most of his fellow manufacturers refused to help him in the fight. In this he had both the courage of his conviction and a veteran knowledge of the ways of rubber supplies and prices. For more than a quarter-century the world prices of natural rubber had careened and spurted. United States rubber manufacturers had faced year's average rubber prices of 98 cents a pound in 1900 – $1.28 in 1905 – $2.06 in 1910 – 66 cents in 1915 – 36 cents in 1920 – and 72 cents in 1925. Significantly, United States rubber manufacturers had consumed 42 percent of the world's production of rubber in 1910, and 70 percent in 1925.

But the problems of rubber supply involved a number of factors that could not be translated into dollar values – or dollar gains or losses. The majority of American rubber manufacturers were inclined to state frankly that they were fabricators, not farmers or foresters – that as factory operators they were resigned to the necessity of paying the prevailing prices for the necessary starting materials.

Mr. Firestone felt differently about it. He knew that the real issue far transcended bank tallies or current fiscal reports. He was intensely aware that the decisive rubber supplies for the United States and all other industrial nations were being concentrated and isolated in far distant tropics whose governments or imperial proprietorships were, as history has now proved, far from infallible; whose labor supplies were not stable; whose top-heavy concentration in one comparatively small sphere of the tropics set up the hazards incident to great distances: ruinous wars, their complex logistics, overextended sea lanes that no navy or combination of navies could conceivably defend. It was clearly possible, even probable, that the rubber supply of the principal rubber-manufacturing nation might be cut off, and clearly evident that an industrial nation without rubber was little better off than the same nation without steel.

As the 1920s progressed, the true nature of the natural-rubber supply situation began to show more clearly. Britain's Crown Colony of Singapore and the Federated Malay States were well established as the majority yielders of natural rubber. Malaya had extremely cheap labor imported from India and China. Practically all Malayan rubber groves were of seedling Hevea, with comparatively meager yields of latex. But with labor cheap and plentiful, and consistent planter advantage in land tenure, an annual crop of 300 pounds of dry rubber per acre was extraordinarily profitable to its proprietor since growing natural rubber at 72 cents a pound was like growing corn at $5 a bushel or cotton at $300 a bale.

The associated British growers elected to disregard Dutch rubber-growing "as a minor and nondecisive competition." But Dutch colonial companies and private planters of the Netherlands Indies, particularly of Sumatra, were actually launching formidable competition. From Amsterdam to Palembang and beyond, the Dutch were going in for rubber. Fine crop experiment stations in Java were beginning to develop and prove unique, high-yielding clones of Hevea trees. In the great jungle frontiers of Sumatra hundreds of thousands of acres of new lands were being cleared and planted to high-yielding rubber, in considerable part with low-wage labor recruited in southern China and equally low-wage workers recruited from the swarming human surpluses of Java.

On both sides of the Pacific informed observers were beginning to agree that the Dutch were proving themselves the ablest of all tropical agronomists and incidentally were proving that the Hevea tree responds particularly well to improved care and the techniques of upbreeding. Meanwhile South America's wild-rubber industry had dwindled to a pitifully feeble trickle. Jungle-pallid *serenguieros* were abandoning the river-edge *estrados* of wild Hevea trees. The tapping trails had grown to tall bush or surrendered to encroaching swamps. The struggling Philippine government was enacting land-limitation laws which discouraged or prohibited the development of large rubber plantations in those islands even though the planting of rubber trees was being expanded in Ceylon, Borneo, and other hot wet islands.

All the while Africa's score in rubber production had remained discouragingly low. In Uganda, Kenya, Sierra Leone, Nigeria, and the Gold Coast, and in scattered locales of French West and French Equatorial Africa, comparatively small plantings of Brazilian-born Hevea trees had appeared. But whether taken singly or collectively these developments were not impressive, and they were not changing the prevailing pattern of British-dominated rubber supply. Rubber crops from the lobelia vine (which is indigenous to Equatorial Africa) and the guayule bush (native to the dry plateaus of Mexico) held market ratings, but practically speaking they were of no real importance. All the rubber grown in Equatorial Africa could not have supplied any major rubber factory.

During the 1920's, that period which Mr. Westbrook Pegler had pertly labeled The Era of Wonderful Nonsense, the United States generally was blanketed by a fog of isolationism. Our people were resentful of such 19-karat phrases as "making the world safe for democracy" and "the war to end wars." World War I had left us a creditor nation, but our allies were not paying their borrowings in money and our government opposed or prohibited repayment in trade. Our foreign trade therefore slipped to an ever-diminishing fraction of the national income. There followed a convenient, inexpensive, and highly vocal aversion to "imperialism"—a distinctly malleable word. The charge of "imperialism" was directed particularly toward American-financed enterprises in small and remote countries, not toward the overwhelming majority of American foreign investments in the industrial nations of Europe. And the word "imperialism" remained in convenient disrepute. America was for Americans. Other countries were for other peoples. The poor picturesque tropics were therefore at liberty to starve, rot of disease, or sweat and bleed in their unaided struggle against lethal environments, or to scream under the lashes or die from the bullets of unscrupulous alien exploiters. We were for us, and our selfishness was not at all enlightened.

Harvey S. Firestone was thoroughly aware of the growing problem of supply, and eager to gain an openly competitive supply of natural rubber. He knew he could retain his place in the American rubber industry by quietly putting up with the cartel setup. Already two prominent American rubber companies, Goodyear and United States Rubber, were developing important Hevea rubber plantations in Malaya and Sumatra, and other American firms were considering the development of rubber plantations. But the truth stood that so long as these American-operated plantations were members of, or parties to, arbitrary cartel domination, they were not solving the crucial problems of rubber supply.

Firestone had stated his convictions both in and out of the councils of American rubber manufacturers, but for the most part his arguments had been ridiculed or ignored. Firestone, however, had both energy and tenacity. He proposed to launch a venture in a tropical country friendly to the United States and free of foreign domination; there to develop areas of rubber with the help of citizen labor (rather than to import alien coolie labor, as had been done in Malaya, Sumatra, and most other rubber-growing centers); to produce rubber competitively with other rubber-growing areas; and not to molest the sovereignty or the economic balance of the country selected.

As they say in Akron, that was a big order. But the need was also big. Synthetic rubber remained unproved. Like steel, rubber had become a primary international commodity. For the best of natural reasons the United States cannot grow its own rubber within home boundaries. Yet American needs for rubber goods continued to soar. By 1924 rubber was filling more than 13,000 staple uses and the United States was importing about 430,000 long tons per year, roughly 92 percent of it from the Far Pacific tropics.

Harvey S. Firestone began dispatching field parties to look for possible sites for Hevea rubber in Central America, South America, and the Far Pacific tropics. He commissioned his eldest son, Harvey S. Firestone, Jr., to investigate the opportunities in various tropical areas. The younger Firestone traveled far – to Ceylon, Singapore, the Netherlands Indies, the Philippines, Sarawak, and farther – to determine where Americans could best produce their own rubber. Some of the areas had evident advantages; all had evident disadvantages.

Graduate of Princeton and youthful veteran of the U. S. Naval Aviation Corps of World War I, the younger Firestone searched far and diligently, calling at many tropical capitals and cooling his heels (and often his enthusiasm) at the inevitable succession of government offices. To the audible disgust of a number of interested onlookers, the Firestones announced that they proposed to grow rubber in West

Africa – in the unique, remote, and controversial Republic of Liberia, where the Firestone company had received the privilege of leasing up to a million acres for a period of ninety-nine years. President C. D. B. King of the Republic confirmed the announcement and pointed out that the arrangement had been granted by the Liberian legislature in session assembled.

Had the location been established on the moon, the announcement could scarcely have created greater astonishment within the rubber industry. To most temperate-zone peoples the African republic had remained a sort of Land of Oz. Previously the rubber industry had taken for granted that Liberia was simply not "rubber country," and there had never been a thorough commercial survey of the interior.

Shipping men and travelers recalled the green, rolling coastline of the country and said that, like most of West Africa, Liberia lacked deep-water ports. British shippers and trading firms, particularly the Elder Dempster Line and Lever Brothers' United Africa Company, had expended some effort in exploiting the more accessible sea-front. In general, the ministers, consuls, and chargés d'affaires functioned not unhappily in the leisure of the little capital, Monrovia. Houseboys, garbed in British-style tropical shorts and singlets, plodded the footways bearing postageless notes (often balanced on the bearer's head and weighted down with a rock). There were a few bicycles, but no oxen, horses, motorcars, or trains.

Road-building had been started in 1916, when a crated Ford automobile consigned to Lagos (the British Crown Colony down the coast) was delivered by lighter, and error, to Monrovia. In regular course the Model-T estray came into the keeping of Colonel Harry W. McBride, of the U. S. State Department, at the time Acting Minister. Assisted by his houseboys and messengers, none of whom had ever seen an automobile, Colonel McBride uncrated the vehicle, assembled it, filled the tank with petrol procured from a passing ship, and after much sweating and cranking succeeded in starting Monrovia's first automobile. He remembered that there were no streets over which to drive this welcome error of cargo-lading, and Liberia's president authorized clearing a first street for the first auto to run on. Thus the auto age came to Liberia.

The entry of the rubber industry was about as sudden. Speaking from Akron, Harvey S. Firestone explained that he had chosen Liberia as a new source of natural rubber "free of foreign domination . . . because of its friendly government and population, having strong natural ties with the United States." He added: "We believe that the world need for rubber can bring Liberia an opportunity for economic development on a large scale. . . . We are trying to understand the Liberian native, for his benefit and our own. He has a good disposition and is naturally adapted to agricultural work. We seek to respect his customs and avoid any derangement of his usual life."

Anybody with experience in tropical work knows that planting rubber trees involves a costly, toilsome, and sometimes hazardous struggle in the primeval jungle. The planter must wait about seven years before the Hevea trees reach a profitable bearing age. The labor needs are great — an average of at least one full-time worker per acre for planting, and at least one permanent worker to every three acres for gathering the crop.

Previously for year after year thousands of the best workers from many of the Liberian tribes had been recruited to work beyond Liberian boundaries, particularly for British plantations and mines in Sierra Leone and the

Gold Coast. Once, several hundred other Liberians, for the most part Kru tribesmen, had been recruited and taken as contract labor to Spain's cacao-growing island of Fernando Po. That action, and the interpretation of it abroad, proved most unfortunate for Liberia.

Brows in several colonial offices had arched when Harvey S. Firestone had said, "I believe that Liberia will now develop faster than any other of the African colonies. . . . A new market will be opened for American goods. It will be an important market. . . . [Heretofore] the only goods that the natives received were sold by European traders. These men commonly charged all that the traffic would bear. We will establish stores to sell American goods at the lowest prices. . . .

"We are interested in any undertaking for the betterment of Liberian life. Sanitation, education, and medical assistance have a prominent place in our program because we understand that the future of the country and of our own enterprise depends upon the education, health, and general welfare of the Liberian people."

In African affairs, such public statements were unprecedented. During a decade in which American businesses had not been inclined to consider proprietary ventures in tropical agriculture, a decade when the colonial policies of Britain, France, and Holland were being drastically merged and fortified by official support from the home capitals, Firestone's launching of such an independent tropical enterprise seemed extreme – or at least exceptional. The company did not seek to exclude any other concession that the Liberian Government might desire to grant. It agreed to employ Liberian citizens to build dwellings, roads, and many other costly installations; it agreed also to pay annual rentals on lands, excises on harvests, and certain other taxes.

Within a year Firestone workers were surveying and building Liberia's first public highway and were marking out two rubber-plantation centers: one above and inland from Monrovia; the other at Cape Palmas on the French Ivory Coast frontier about 225 miles south and east. Within three years a first 30,000 acres of the jungle and bush lands were cleared and planted to Hevea trees. Coastal ships were operating between the two plantation centers. First automobiles and trucks were appearing on the newly opened roads. Motorboats and barges were joining native canoes along the meandering rivers to the interior. A Diesel electric plant was providing the first rural electrification known to the area. Native carpenters, abetted by company-built sawmills, machine shops, and brick and cement yards, were building homes and offices. Liberia's first radio-telegraph station was in operation.

With Firestone help, the Harvard School of Tropical Medicine was beginning extensive investigations of tropical diseases in Liberia. The newly formed Firestone Plantations Company had built, equipped, staffed, and put in operation a first field hospital and field clinic for treating native workers and effecting field sanitation. By 1928, the plantations company was working with various Liberian mission centers and Dr. James L. Sibley, then educational adviser of the Liberian Government, to implement a coöperative plan for providing more educational facilities for the new plantations and the country as a whole. Harvey S. Firestone noted: "We have undertaken as our special part of the [educational] program to establish trade schools, where young Liberians will be trained in the mechanical crafts. Already we have been able to teach the adult Liberian how to drive an automobile and carry on certain mechanical work. . . ."

The renewed saga of Americans at work in far places had roused highly varied comments. But the fact stood that the largest American enterprise in all Africa had been launched energetically and forthrightly.

Time and the tropics were writing a new and bizarre story.

Chapter Six

The Changing Industry of Natural Rubber

UNTIL 1925 the great majority of Liberians had never seen a Hevea tree, and like most other peoples they were unaware of certain epoch-making changes in an epoch-making crop. In 1875 Sir Henry Wickham, amateur botanist and professional soldier of fortune, collected some 70,000 seed of wild Hevea trees along the Tapajos River in frontier Brazil, and stealthily dispatched them to the greenhouses of England's own Kew, where the resulting 2,800 seedling trees were nurtured tenderly and presently transplanted by dribbles to Ceylon and other Eastern hot spots; but since that time no other such important events had occurred in rubber-growing.

By 1928 the original Wickham seedlings had produced hundreds of millions of descendants in the Far East tropics, thereby enabling Britannia to rule the rubber supply for a period. But meanwhile skillful Dutch agronomists and plant breeders, having observed that certain seedling Hevea trees produced several times as much latex as near-by trees of approximately the same age and size and type, had employed the creative intricacies of selection, cross pollination, and other strategies of tree breeding to evolve reasonably staple Hevea clones which permitted a given plantation to produce several times as much latex as another planted to unselected seedling stocks.

In one decade of experimental work, the able Dutch geneticists and experiment-station workers of Sumatra and Java had pushed far ahead in the adaptation of jungle-born Hevea to orderly and practical forestry. In Sumatra alone almost three-quarters of a million acres of the higher-yielding clonal rubber was at or near bearing age by the end of 1928. By then the Netherlands Indies, which in 1920 had produced barely one-twelfth of the world's rubber supply, was producing an important part of it. As the Stevenson Plan continued to waver more and more shakily, the Dutch prospects for becoming a power in the rubber-control agreement were improving. Britain no longer ruled rubber.

At any time during the late 1920s almost any crystal-gazer could have foreseen stormy weather for the rubber trade. Despite all the would-be ingenious controls, the world prices of rubber were beginning to wobble. Not far distant were the furies of world depression, the slackening of industrial demands, and the dismal drop of rubber values to an average during 1930 of 10.2 cents a pound and once to an all-time low of three cents during the same year. This was in contrast to the earlier world prices of 98 cents a pound, then 36 cents, 20 cents, then $2.07, and at one time (1912) to a record high of $3 per pound.

Any experienced farmer respects the work, sweat, planning, and combined efforts that are required to produce an annual crop. Natural rubber is laborious and perennial, a lifetime crop. The ordinary farmer's opportunity to take a breathing spell in the temperate-zone winter to study the faults and merits of the crops just made, and to plan better crops for the growing season immediately ahead, is denied the rubber planter. He has no vacations. His work is a merging of farming, forestry, and long-term investment, of work routines that cover a fourth to a third of a century or longer. All mistakes and omissions are proportionately costly. And successful rubber-growing calls as well for the simultaneous development of a sound subsistence agriculture.

When Harvey S. Firestone, the resolute individualist, had declared that "Americans should produce their own rubber," he evidently knew, in a general way, what such an exhortation implied. When he chose Liberia as the particular locale for producing an independent rubber supply, he required the ability in his staff members to fit the needs and the progress of a rapidly changing Hevea agronomy and forestry into the unique economy, folk life, and primitive subsistence agriculture of interior Liberia. It was not enough to establish Hevea rubber trees as a principal Liberian crop. The real challenge was to coördinate rubber with other essential crops, to fit rubber into the social and economic life of a primitive agricultural country.

The earlier expedients of many other rubber lands were barred. For example, the mass importation of experienced plantation labor by contract — as practiced in most other rubber-producing areas — was not to be imposed upon Liberia. The Firestone desire to respect the tribal integrity and folk resources of the native Liberian people was "radical" in the sense that it was so largely unprecedented.

Labor was and always will be the first need of natural rubber. It was and is necessary to recruit Liberian labor in keeping with the tradition, authority, and manpower of the respective tribes. The chief still gives permission for tribe members to work the rubber. Inevitably it is desirable to house the workers as they are accustomed to being housed — in approximate replicas of native villages.

The new rubber planters and engineers from Ohio, Virginia, Pennsylvania, and a dozen other untropical places led inexperienced workers into the roadless, jungle-littered valleys and hills. With native labor they began building a succession of villages and towns for the necessary thousands of plantation workers. By now there are about 7,500 thatched huts, each providing quarters for at least four people; about 1,000 brick houses; office buildings, stores, commissaries, latex stations, and plantation factories; about 80 homes for the executive personnel (somewhat like California ranch houses); port buildings, town houses, and other constructions: altogether the housing equivalent of an American city of 25,000 to 30,000 people.

Housing is a continuing obligation. But sufficient nourishing food for the labor was actually the number-one problem. The Liberian people have long used rice, traditionally grown, harvested, processed, and cooked, as their staff of life. The people also require protein foods, particularly meats. But inasmuch as their eating habits are traditional and therefore decidedly inflexible, changes of diet, if effected at all, must be effected cautiously and with subtle diplomacy. In considerable part the pioneers learned this the hard and expensive way.

For example, in the early days of the Firestone venture a well-intentioned manager decided to benefit his workers by serving them breakfast in the field. The rubber-tappers' work day necessarily begins at dawn. Confident that a good hearty breakfast would help them through the long morning, and forgetting that the tribesmen simply do not eat a hearty breakfast — as a rule they eat no breakfast at all — the manager had the entire work force gathered in the compound and issued an early morning feast of boiled rice, smoked fish, and palm-nut gravy. Having gorged themselves, the workers strolled dazedly into the rubber groves, but, finding themselves much too full to work, they picked cool shady spots and promptly went to sleep.

The Firestone men instituted weekly rice issues, delivering to each worker a prescribed allotment of the basic food grain: as a rule, sixteen pounds weekly for all workers with wives, eight pounds for single men, and 24 to 32 pounds for the headmen or native foremen. This calls for large-scale procurement of rice and for painstaking study of the basic economy of the land and the people. In order to avert the local and frequently violent inflations in rice prices and to protect the workers and the tribesmen generally from the ruinous rice famines that have repeatedly harassed the interior, the company began the methodical purchase and storage of Liberian-grown rice, which they supplemented as needs required with shiploads of rice imported from Siam, Ceylon, India, and other rice-exporting countries.

But the undertaking immediately brought to light the need for better control of rice prices. At a time when the local prices of rice were averaging around three cents a pound, the Firestone planters established a ceiling of two and a half cents a pound for all rice sold to their workers. Invariably at a loss to the company (recently in the face of international rice prices ranging from seven to nine or more cents a pound, and Liberian prices averaging five cents) they have resolutely maintained the first ceiling price for all rice issued to workers. This price ceiling proves indispensable as a defense against the disastrous inflations that are chronic in the greater part of Equatorial Africa. Not even the lushest and most primeval jungle can withstand unregulated profit-grabbing on the sale of basic foods. When left alone the local prices of native or "country rice" are prone to slump to ruinous lows of a cent a pound or less. At such prices tribe-grown surpluses of rice are scarcely worth carrying to markets. Time and again good grain has been left to shatter in the fields or to mold and weevil under leaky thatched roofs because low prices took away all incentive for marketing the crop. On the other hand, when a rice crop is poor or fails completely in a given backwoods area the countryside prices soar beyond all reason and poor people go hungry. Repeatedly the inflation of rice prices has forced entire clans or tribes to set out on desperate, uneconomic migrations.

The Firestone men did not attempt to grow rice as a company crop, but they have been and are still able to supply most of the necessary rice issues with grain purchased directly from the tribal farmers. This helps to stabilize and improve the native agronomy of rice, and by providing an active local market it provides the incentive for bigger rice-plantings.

The possibility of a rice famine remains the worst dread of the inland tribesmen. As recently as 1943 a severe rice shortage in various inland areas caused the Liberian Government to request all tribal chiefs to coöperate in a campaign to double the rice-plantings of the interior to protect the tribespeople against hunger.

The backcountry Liberians are inveterate rice eaters, invariably preferring it to wheat, corn, or any other grain. Fortunately, the home-husked, unpolished rice of Liberia is exceptionally nutritious and palatable. As in most tropical countries, the prevailing price of the staple food effectively controls the real value of wages. This fact was proved anew during the years of World War II. For example, in Nigeria (Liberia's big and near neighbor, a British-mandated territory with about thirty million tribespeople) the war brought about a virtual collapse of tribal economy. Cassava, fish, and palm oils are the basic foods here. Under colonial regulations effected during the war years, the United Africa Company and other British-owned commissaries and stores were permitted to raise prices of staple merchandise approximately 40 percent and to make additional rises as the supplies grew scarcer.

But the common labor wage of Nigeria stayed at about one shilling or 22 cents a day. With wage levels frozen, the price of a shirt leaped to 25 shillings, fresh fish soared to a shilling a pound, and prices of cassava root quadrupled. Palm oils and palm kernels are Nigeria's principal export and credit base. During World War I palm-oil prices had soared to £50 a ton. During World War II the British Government, desperately in need of palm oils for war manufactures, established a ceiling of £11 sterling per ton. His Majesty's men sought to get out more of the oil by introducing kerosene to the outlying tribes, since as a rule a considerable part of the palm oil harvested by an average tribe family is used for lamp fuel. American oil companies delivered the kerosene at a Nigerian port for about five cents a gallon. But colonial duties average twenty cents a gallon and inland delivery costs raised the tally until the price of kerosene exceeded that of palm oil. This meant, of course, that edible oils continued to light most of the lamps of Nigeria. And what is much more unfortunate, the colony has suffered an apparently interminable series of paralyzing strikes and public protests, all in support of the proposition that a predatory and uncontrolled economy no longer fits even the simplest of agrarian tropics.

In Liberia the Firestone method began to prove itself a stabilizer for domestic rice production. Even during the prolonged upsets resulting from World War II, Liberia has remained free of the riots, paralyzing strikes, and other troubles of colonial Africa; this despite the fact that rubber promptly became the decisive cash crop of the country. The Firestone operations showed that price stability of rice made for integrity of buying power, and that paying bonuses for superior work was particularly beneficial to tribal workers, most of whom like to work as groups or teams rather than as individuals.

But the introduction of rubber raised many other questions. In considerable part these bear on the eternal problem of adequate nutrition for tropical peoples. Rice, the basic food of Liberia, even when eaten with palm oil, the principal source of fat, cannot provide an entirely sufficient diet. More protein foods, particularly meat, are needed. But livestock remains extremely scarce throughout the country. By tradition and age-old practice the jungle wild life has supplied most or all of the meat diet. Inevitably, however, the clearing and planting of the jungles upsets and shifts the habits of native animals. Inevitably, too, concentrating the work population accentuates the need for meat. The meat supply has therefore become a foremost concern in fitting Hevea rubber into an integrated agriculture.

Cattle and draft animals, however, particularly oxen and horses, are chronic sufferers from sleeping sickness as well as from the scarcity of pastures and of grains other than rice. Insidiously the tsetse fly continues to plunge the micro-organisms of the dreaded sleeping sickness into the bloodstreams of the larger domestic animals. In Liberia, as elsewhere, there are many livestock diseases, but sleeping sickness is by far the most damaging. Time and again it has decimated herds of cattle and debilitated valuable wild animals like antelope and deer.

Through generations and centuries the tribal Liberians have depended primarily on wild animals and fish for their protein foods. In general the elephants, bush cows, antelopes, deer, and monkeys are the most important meat providers. A few half-wild hogs forage in the open country without being fed by man. On the limited pasture lands that adjoin some towns and villages one sees the dwarfish native cattle—darkish, pigmy-sized bovines which have somehow developed resistance to sleeping sickness; but they do not give milk. Chickens are the best-established and most useful domestic fowl, but as a rule they produce few eggs.

The age-old proposition remains that when and if game is plentiful, rice abundant, and hunters diligent and well armed, there is usually meat. But when times are hard, when great floods or storms occur, or when locusts sweep over the garden-sized farms or voracious birds or mischievous elephants wipe out the rice fields, then famine comes. Fatalistically the tribesman is prone to eat well when food is plentiful, and when famine comes he avoids starvation by nibbling bark and roots.

Obviously all of this means that the rich, tree-crowded earth of Africa must somehow be utilized to feed its people better. Liberia today is the only rubber-producing country —probably the only country in the world—where for three days' pay the rubber tapper can buy outright an acre of fertile land. But rubber is stubbornly inedible, and the food problem has long been the nemesis of successful rubber forestry.

Firestone sought a remedy for this shortcoming. As the blocks of clearings and plantings increased, it instituted a program for research and experimentation with subsistence crops. Since 1931 the research center near Harbel* has grown to be one of the most efficient in West Africa. Staffed by a group of highly qualified agronomists, pathologists, botanists, and chemists, this research center supplements studies of production, upbreeding, bacterial control, and processing of natural rubber with experi-

---

*About 45 miles inland from Monrovia.

mental and practical plantings of various tropical fruits, palm trees, and vegetable crops, imported as well as native; and field crops, timbers, and soil-saving cover crops. The experiments with fruits—particularly mangoes, papayas, mangosteens, pineapples, plantains, bananas, and avocados (in Liberia, "butter pears")—prove that the soils and climates are generally suited to most of the edible tropical fruits and to many of the palm crops, particularly African oil palm. Experimental plantings of such valuable tropical timbers as teak and Australian fir have been successful, though not impressive as competitors of the towering native forests.

The planting experiments have proved that sugar canes grow well and that sugar can be produced cheaply in the preponderantly deep and fertile soil. The same holds for bamboo, some varieties of which can be made valuable as suppliers of fences, furniture, and flooring, as pipe substitutes, and for other real needs of tropical peoples. Such tropical fiber crops as jute, roselle, and abacá flourish. Derris, a Malayan root crop that provides rotenone, one of the most valuable of insecticides, shows good promise as a supplementary crop. Citrus productions, particularly of oranges and grapefruit, is highly promising. Bananas grow well and yield abundantly.

A number of the common garden vegetables, including squashes, cabbages, and tomatoes, show decided promise. Sweet potatoes, yams, and peanuts are already established as food crops. But, as in most other tropical countries, the growing of green vegetables is difficult. Only elevated planting beds can provide sufficient drainage, even during the twice-a-year merging of the wet and dry seasons which is the best time for gardening. Some types of edible beans grow well in Liberia; other valuable vegetables including various shell beans, peas, potatoes, root vegetables, and sweet corns are not yet staple to Liberian fields or gardens. Firestone agronomists have made considerable progress in developing an edible rice bean as a cover crop for the rubber groves. But all the prospective or new crops require painstaking and elaborate adaptation, upbreeding, and protection from local natural enemies.

The planting of the big groves of rubber trees stressed the importance of craft skills, and the development of Hevea rubber as a principal export crop established an increasing demand for native carpenters and blacksmiths, and for local lumber mills, brick yards, and many other native enterprises. But the enduring life of Liberia continues agricultural, and subsistence agriculture remains the indispensable factor.

From Firestone's beginning in Liberia, experimentation has proved that the problems of developing good and plentiful livestock to supply meat, milk, cheese, and other protein foods remain far more difficult than those of developing better and diverse vegetable crops. Sickly livestock are still common in most tropical countries, and imported purebred cattle rarely survive. Some livestock experts believe that it might be possible to import pregnant heifers whose offspring would provide a first native generation of purebred cattle with some measure of adaptation to Liberian environment. Others contend that, by prolonged experiments in selecting and breeding the better specimens of native cattle and other livestock, favorable grades would eventually result. Even so, there are certain prerequisites to developing a beef or milk supply for inland Liberia: the introduction of needed feed grains and grasses, improved pastures, dependable water supplies, and sustained warfare against the tsetse fly.

Aware of this, Firestone established and began to operate a central livestock farm near Harbel. By gradual stages this farm has been stocked with cattle (all native "grade" animals); sheep (the typical woolless sheep of the African tropics); hogs (American Durocs, Berkshires, and crosses thereof); a flock of chickens (White Leghorns and barred Plymouth Rocks); and a number of meat rabbits.

The results grow more encouraging with passing time. Of this livestock the chickens and rabbits appear to be the most promising for the immediate protein needs of the tribespeople. Though the hogs breed and thrive reasonably well and produce edible pork, the practical growing of swine is handicapped by lack of suitable feeds, particularly corn, for which peanuts, cassava, and palm nuts are of necessity the local substitutes. The sheep show considerable promise as meat animals, but they do not thrive on the local range so well as the small, short-haired native goats which more and more of the tribespeople are raising as meat animals. The cattle, typical of their kind, are small, rarely dressing more than 500 pounds. Even so, they are a valuable source of beef and leather, though not of milk.

The work in poultry-growing is particularly promising for the tropics, where egg production ordinarily averages no more than one-third of the prevailing averages in the United States. As a rule, too, eggs hatch poorly in the tropics. But at present the incubation rate at the Harbel hatchery is approximately average for the United States. The record of the laying flock is around 140 eggs yearly per hen, which is at least fair for laying flocks in the United States, and is outstandingly good for tropics. However, the experiment in poultry and egg production continues to show that feeding is the primary consideration. In the tribe home very little food is thrown away, and by ancient tradition rice, the great staple, is for people, not to be fed to fowl or animals. For that reason some of the meat breeds of hares that can forage for themselves in the open suggest promise as a first source of domestic livestock.

In general, experienced Liberian farmers assert that the feat of developing an adequate meat supply is possible. Liberia is part of Equatorial Africa, and the fact stands that in near-by areas cattle-growing is succeeding despite tsetse flies, grain shortages, scarcity of pastures, and the many previous failures.

For example, in Nigeria one can see how the Fulami tribespeople have lately built up a highly successful and indigenous dairy industry. The latter has required a great many years of experiment and devoted work on the part of tribe members and their chiefs. But the efforts have succeeded — not only in Nigeria but in great areas of French West Africa and certain British African possessions. Successful dairy depots and creameries continue to appear in many parts of West and Central Africa, particularly in the Congo, Uganda, and Kenya — successes that have been made possible by improved cattle husbandry, better veterinary services, better pastures and water supplies, the expansion of grain crops, and most of all by the painstaking and devoted work of tribespeople in shaping farm enterprises to fit local needs. Invariably as the ventures succeed, the local demands for livestock products promptly rise.

Fortunately and exceptionally, the Liberian rubber worker maintains ties with his home soil and his tribe. He remains a tribesman, working for himself and his tribe under the auspices of his chief. He is not a coolie "signed up" to spend many years in alien rubber groves. The rubber groves are as much a bona fide part of Liberia as are the men and the boys who work them. The facts that some 140 citizen farmers of Liberia are now growing Hevea rubber as a proprietary crop, and that many or most of the independently owned rubber plantations show promise of durable success, spotlight the Hevea tree as a valid, national crop.

Like the tribes and the drums, Hevea rubber trees are now part of Liberia. Their productive life is drawn from Liberian earth and sun and rain and workmen. But the Hevea crop can continue to succeed only as the more primary agriculture of Liberia succeeds. Competent workers can be drawn only from a well-fed and healthy population. Interdependence is the theme of work. Whatever soundly benefits the tribes benefits the natural rubber industry, the Liberian government, and all Liberia; not to mention the United States of America.

Along with its many changes and experiments, the industry of natural rubber keeps to a steadfast routine. Behind the technologies and complexities of producing natural rubber is the fundamental routine of operation.

As a rule, after five or six years of field growth the Hevea trees are "ripe" for tapping. A "tappable" tree should have a man's-waist-height diameter of at least five inches. The young trees are mapped, and numbered by rows; and tapping panels are precisely marked, at thirty-degree angles, preferably on the north side of the tree and at a height of about 50 inches above ground. The tapping panels are usually marked with patterns cut from tin or other light metal. The new groves are divided into "tasks" (tapping assignments) of from 250 to 300 trees each. All this is incidental to the tapping, which is the repetitive, enduring life of natural rubber.

Tapping is probably the most difficult and exacting of

all harvests. It calls for extraordinary skill and almost infinite patience on the part of the tappers. The precise routines vary somewhat with work forces, weather, and type of rubber tree involved. But in general the day-in, day-out chore of collecting the milky white latex is more or less this: The work begins early — preferably immediately after daybreak, since the milky latex runs best before the intensely hot part of the tropical day. Particularly in fair weather a Hevea tree usually yields its stint of latex between dawn and eleven in the morning, when the increasing heat causes the latex to coagulate. But the hours between six and ten are best. By eleven, sometimes sooner, the "bleeding" of the milky white latex begins to slow.

Pounding the "morning gong" sounds the muster. From the thatched villages the tappers proceed to their tasks, each man or boy equipped with a tapping knife which has a sharp, rounded blade protruding from the base of a heavy wooden handle. As a rule each tapper has two large stainless-steel buckets (holding either sixteen or thirty-two quarts) which he carries on a shoulder yoke or "picul stick," a bottle of "chemical water" or anticoagulant, and a bag for collecting the coagulum and ground scrap drippings from the previous day's tapping.

After the tree has been tapped and the fresh latex collected, the tapping wound remains coated with a hardened coagulum of latex which stays until the next tapping round. Smaller quantities of the tree milk spill out on near-by bark areas of the tree. Sometimes, too, the latex drips into untended cups and there becomes coagulated from contact with the warm air and the latter's ever dense population of bacteria. "Natural coagulation" also occurs when latex adheres to metal surfaces or when catch cups overflow. This "off-grade" rubber is systematically collected and processed, since when properly attended to it fills various worth-while commercial uses; and when improperly attended to it causes serious injury by contaminating the primary supply.

The tapper carries other useful articles: panel patterns, bits of cord, nails with especially sharpened points for outlining the panel or measuring bark depths before cutting or "wounding" the tree, a file and a whetstone for sharpening his tapping knife, and a glass bottle for carrying the fungicide used for washing or disinfecting tree wounds. Each tree is individually equipped with a latex catch cup made of glass, clay, chinaware, or aluminum (at present glass cups are preferred); a "hanger wire," a smooth steel wire that holds the catch cup in position immediately below the tapping panel; and a small spout that directs the latex into the cup.

In the partial shade of the rubber groves one is only vaguely aware of the many gadgets that are needed in harvesting the white latex that presently changes to stretchy rubber. But at plantation storages or division headquarters one sees miniature mountains of catch cups, tapping knives, and various other accessories; high mounds of smooth wire; and great circles of workers pounding the wire into "tree clamps" for holding the cups in place. The procurement and replacement of tapping equipment is an unending task.

Out in the groves one appreciates the fact that the tapper is the truly indispensable man of rubber. In final analysis the life and value of any Hevea property must be measured in terms of the precious tree bark. The tapper is the custodian of that bark; his hands, his two eyes, and his skill determine the producing life of the tree.

The latex oozes out of a layer of cells located immediately below the outer bark but above the cambium layer of the tree. Each time the cambium layer is cut or broken, the tree is injured—permanently and more or less seriously injured. If the tapper's knife cuts too deeply, he wounds and injures the tree; if not deeply enough, the latex will not "bleed" in sufficient quantity. His skill must enable him to cut within a measured distance of no more than one millimeter (about the thickness of an ordinary sheet of writing paper).

Even with the best possible tapping, the precious tree bark is consumed at the rate of about one inch a month – roughly one-sixteenth of an inch for each tapping. (Usually each tree is tapped every second day.) As a rule the original tapping panel is placed halfway around the tree. If the tapping is done well, the depleted bark renews itself after five years or so, and thus by means of systematic conservation of the bark the bearing life of a Hevea tree can be extended indefinitely.

The tapper must have varied skills. After he has "put the trees to bleed," he waits for the later morning collection gong, then proceeds to collect the new latex from each cup and to pour it into his buckets, each of which is marked with the number of his task. Usually the tapper collects latex in his smaller (twelve-to-sixteen-quart) bucket, which he presently empties into his big bucket. He also picks up the "ground scrap," "cup washing," "bark scraps," and other debris that contains latex, as well as the already coagulated or lump rubber. He places the recovered rubber in his bag or basket and carries it to the collecting station, along with his bucket or buckets of latex. Arrived at the station he joins the other members of his work gang, and in turn delivers the latex and scrap to a clerk, who weighs and records the day's "get" and strains the fresh latex into a storage tank. Then the tapper washes out his buckets, and finishes his work day by marking trees, chopping "small bush," weeding, repairing trails, pruning trees, washing catch cups, and otherwise maintaining his "task."

But many other talents are required for producing rubber. There are the engineers who survey and supervise the building of the necessary roads, highways, and bridges; the telephonists, machinists, chemists, accountants, and clerks, the bankers who provide routine banking services for plantation employees, and the plantation doctors and surgeons and sanitarians. Also needed are tractor operators, truck and auto mechanics, and garage supervisors.

On the Firestone plantations there are also the drivers of the big trucks with tank trailers that make the daily collections of latex from the plantation division receiving stations and haul it to the central "factory" or processing plant where the latex is reduced to exportable forms of rubber.

Many other skilled and professional workers are required: inspectors, auditors, merchants, commissary managers, plumbers, pipeliners, electricians, sanitarians, "dressers" or medical assistants, blacksmiths, carpenters, and so on through a roster of at least fifty particular trades and skills. But the youthful tappers – the Peter Johnnies, Wantos, Flomos, Gbandi Boys, and Tobios – are the ones who have made Hevea rubber a memorable world crop, and who keep it so.

From time to time new roads push into this frontier and inevitably they change it. Firestone plantations alone have built and opened about 400 miles of primary and secondary roads, principally to link together some 125 square miles of Hevea plantations and to connect the plantations with towns and ports.

Nevertheless, about two-thirds of all Liberia remains beyond the reach of motor roads. In the interior people continue to tramp the meandering trails afoot or to ride in a sack hammock borne on the heads of strong men. The hammock boy, stalwart and deft-footed recipient of a standard wage of twenty cents a day for carrying and five cents a day for return without burden, remains an indispensable citizen of the great green frontiers of Liberia.

Frederick Helm, a veteran jungle trekker from Columbus, Ohio, of Firestone Plantations' labor department and one of the best-informed students of Liberia, reported as follows his latest "bush trip," made in company with Liberia's District Commissioner, R. J. Taylor:

> ". . . The trip was a sort of triumphal procession with a retinue strung out about a quarter of a mile behind us. Word had gone ahead, and at every village there was a large delegation to meet us. Some hunters or ex-soldiers fired old muzzle-loading rifles in salute. The women of the villages all were out singing and dancing as the Commissioner went by. . . . Our following grew with each village . . . until we arrived at N'Dilue where the hammock carriers seemed to take great delight in parading us around through the town, [they] at a dead run.
>
> "That evening the town people staged a show in honor of the District Commissioner. A cow was presented to the Commissioner; there was much drumming, dancing, and feasting. The country devils* in costumes made of green, blue, yellow, and black bird feathers put on a dance that seemed to impress the natives greatly because all during the dance they maintained a very respectful silence. . . . Another interesting dancer was a country devil on stilts. He could take steps about ten feet long, and ran and danced as he did so, displaying a remarkable sense of balance. When he wanted to rest he just sat on top of a native hut. He stood about fifteen feet high,

---

*Local men of magic or witch doctors.

with long trousers all the way to the ground. The women are not allowed to look at the face of this particular devil; he always appears masked in public. On this occasion his mask began to come off and all the women started to run into their houses with a great deal of frantic shouting, until the mask was adjusted. . . .

"The District Commissioner's residence at Voinjama is a large, well-constructed building made of sun-dried brick with a thick thatch roof. The rest of the Government buildings are of the same style. . . . The sun-dried brick are laid up with mud for mortar; if there is sufficient roof overhang so the rain does not beat the walls, they will hold up for a long time.

"From Voinjama we went to Kolahun, and then to Bolahun, where the Fathers of the Episcopal 'Order of the Holy Cross' maintain a Mission. They have a school, a dispensary, and the second largest church building in Liberia. It is a beautiful and well-designed building. . . . From Bolahun we went to Nyakollie to visit Paramount Chief Momo Henna of the Gbande tribe. This is a small town of 54 huts situated on top of a high steep hill. The Chief made me a present of a huge pineapple. Everywhere I went it was the same story as far as workers were concerned: they would send boys as soon as their farm work was finished.

"We started through the Gizzie country to Borlilo, the home of Paramount Chief Quehmorlu of the Gizzies. He received us very well and provided all my boys with ample food and good houses as well as a good house for myself. . . . We always pay for the things provided us, and present the Chief with a gift. Salt is highly prized in the interior, as is also tobacco; shotgun shells make a princely gift. . . . While at Ganta we learned that the Mano word for money is *pehleh* which, translated, means 'things mother.'"

The pattern of Firestone's operations in Liberia is important for future operations by other enterprises in the vast African tropics. The plantation workers, the great majority of whom are tappers, are recruited with the specific permission and by the authority of the chief and the official representative of the Liberian Government. When a new worker arrives, he is assigned a hut, issued rice and incidental supplies, and put on the payroll of a particular plantation division.

Next he is assigned to a Tappers' School. For the purpose, cut Hevea trees are brought together and placed upright in the ground, like posts. An experienced headman or foreman demonstrates, painstakingly instructing each newcomer in the highly skilled fundamentals of rubber-tapping. After the preliminary exercises, the tapper-to-be is assigned to a group of thirty and begins to practice the craft on the producing Hevea trees. Six weeks is the usual tryout period. As a rule the newcomers who cannot qualify as tappers find other plantation work to which they are adapted. Extremely few are misfits in terms of the work, but many become homesick for their homes and relatives back in the tribal villages. According to Firestone records, between 55 and 65 percent of the newcomers from the tribes remain at plantation work for at least a year. Thereafter, the turnover rate is much lower. When the tribesman finally comes to feel at home at plantation work he is likely to stay for a long time.

With the passing years the labor roster has grown. When World War II came to an end, the Firestone Liberian plantations – comprising 45 divisions, of which 35 were developed and 33 were in bearing – were employing 24,490 Liberian citizens as rubber-tappers, supervisors, or foresters; about 900 more in the engineering department; about 1,000 more in the two latex-processing centers; and about 1,300 miscellaneous workers. Supplementing the plantation work forces are the headquarters staffs and a banking staff; in all an executive personnel of about 160. These are principally American-Liberians, United States citizens, and a few Swiss, British, Dutch, and Spaniards.

The Firestone venture was still in the infant stage when the world depression of 1930 arrived. Even in the long-established rubber lands of Malaya, Ceylon, and Sumatra, efficient planting companies strove hard to break even as rubber prices slumped to all-time lows.

The new Liberian plantings were in their most costly years. Because they were pioneering in a tropical enterprise where caution was essential, Firestone planters had started by planting hardy seedling rubber principally from seed imported from Nigeria before the new and higher-yielding Sumatran clones were fully proved. When the great depression struck, the Firestone planters were making good use of bud-grafted or clonal rubber trees.

The world depression was a major blessing to the actual agronomy of Hevea rubber, just as it was to that of bananas, sugar cane, abacá, and many other hot-country crops. For it enforced the mandate of Improve or Quit. The wild-rubber industry became extinct, and in the Eastern tropics an estimated million acres of over-age or inferior Hevea groves were abandoned. Careless or obsolete harvest and processing practices were necessarily dropped.

Far more important was the fact that the depression hastened the development and international acceptance of clonal or selected-strain rubber. In the new rubber lands, just as in the long-established centers, the introduction of higher-yielding strains brought about many improvements in the techniques of tapping, harvesting, and processing the latex of Hevea trees, and in re-estimating their value.

During 1928, Firestone men brought in several dozen of the promising new Hevea clones, developed for the most part in Sumatra or Java. Additional costly and painstaking experimentation was then necessary, since improved Hevea is no easy blessing. Like newly developed breeds or strains of livestock, new varieties of plants frequently show unpredictable or contradictory reactions to alien soils and climates. With time, some of the new clones of Hevea became admirably suited to Liberia. Many others did not. The wood of some proved to be extremely brittle and therefore subject to ruinous wind damage. Others yielded splendidly, but reacted unfavorably to local weather conditions or fungous enemies. There were and are conspicuous physical contrasts among the various clones. Strangely enough, trees of one clone sometimes lean drunkenly, while those of another are exceptionally straight. Contrasts in leaf structure, bark coloration, vitality of seed, and other physical characteristics are strongly marked.

Like purebred domestic livestock, superior rubber trees require prolonged and skillful upbreeding. Moreover, the introduction of clonal rubber greatly increased the importance of nursery management and made skillful bud-grafting an absolute prerequisite to the development of rubber groves.

That "selective breeding" promptly became the slogan of natural-rubber growers is readily understandable. Even in the wilds no two Hevea trees are precisely alike. This, of course, is true of all trees, but Hevea differences and variants are exceptionally pronounced. Some rubber trees are more vigorous than others. Some branch sparingly, others have heavy crowns. Leaf shapes are highly variable. And even in the case of wild or scrub trees the latex yields of individual trees vary enormously.

Before 1920, Dutch agronomists and foresters had proved scientifically that the latex yields and other characteristics of selected seedling trees can be reproduced more or less consistently in the offspring of those trees. Thus, with time and work, the overall yields of an entire grove may be "brought to type" by planting the grove to trees that have resulted from the reproduction of a superior "mother" tree.

However, in order to keep the clone constant the selected tree strains must be reproduced by grafting and not directly from seed. The feat of developing a superior clone of Hevea trees begins with a painstaking survey of the "scrub" or seedling trees. Having selected one or several trees that seem clearly superior to the many, the experimenter removes leafbuds which he grafts on young seedling trees, preferably in a sheltered nursery plot. If, say, ten promising trees are selected, buds from each are grafted on a designated group of young seedling trees, which in time are transplanted to the field and there let grow to bearing age. After seven or eight years, the experimenter compares the clones thus developed on a basis of latex yields, resistance to storms and to diseases, rate and symmetry of growth, overall hardiness, and other characteristics. With still more time and work, he selects the superior grafted trees as "mother trees" to newer and perhaps still better clones or strains. But the experimenter is obliged to remember that a good clone for one area or grove is not necessarily a good clone for another.

Cross-pollination is a method of tree-breeding devised to establish a source of seeds capable of reproducing consistent similarity between seedling and parent trees. For this intricate work the tree breeder usually builds a platform about the chosen mother tree and waits for the pale yellow Hevea flowers — homely but perfumed — to appear. To effect the cross-pollination he encloses each blossom panicle in a tiny cellophane bag just before the emergence of the pistillate flower. On the following day when the flowers have opened within the bag, the breeder removes the bag and rubs the stigmatic surfaces of the chosen blossoms with the anthers of the desired staminate parent. After effecting the pollination, he inserts small plugs of cotton in the calyxes of the pistillate flowers to prevent accidental or uncontrolled pollination, removes all the undeveloped flowers, then numbers and tags the pistillate flowers and records the names of the parent trees. Such work is tedious and exacting. Sometimes it proves brilliantly successful; more frequently it does not.

Clonal rubber, wherein the living bud of a high-yielding tree is made the aboveground complement of hardy seedling roots, came to Liberia within a decade after it had been born and proved in Sumatra. The change is now obvious to the eye. As one walks in the new and well-ordered forest of rubber trees, he learns to recognize by sight, sometimes by smell, the always distinguishable Hevea clones. For example, there is *Avros 49* (the word "Avros" is made from the initials of five tongue-wrenching Dutch names), a fast-growing tree with a leaning trunk, smooth gray bark, and dense shade. The clone is a good yielder. But it is inclined to drip its latex slowly — latex that for some wholly unexplained cause is considerably below average in its content of dry rubber. On the other hand, *Avros 50* is a still more handsome tree, exceptionally straight, thin-crowned, and highly resistant to wind. It yields well and its latex is well above average in content of dry rubber. Today *Avros 50* is one of Liberia's best clones. A close relative, *Avros 256,* immensely successful in Sumatra, has failed in Liberia.

Bodjong Datar 5 is a straight tree that grows slowly, is highly wind-resistant, has excellent bark renewal, and, in Liberia, is another of the better-producing clones. *Bodjong*

Datar 10, also a splendid yielder of latex, grows rapidly but has a large crown that is highly susceptible to wind damage. *Tjirandji 16* has a soft bark of medium thickness, a large and well-shaped crown, and fairly straight and well-rounded trunk that leans slightly as a result of prevailing wind direction. *Prang Besar 186* is a vigorous tree with obliquely erect branches and a soft bark that is easily tapped. It is highly wind-resistant and usually above average in its production of latex.

So the clones and clonal habits vary. Still better clones wait to be developed, and indeed are being developed. Any synthetic-rubber factory that can keep pace with this improvement of Hevea trees is indeed a remarkable factory, highly inventive and efficient.

The coming of the clone changed the grove or forest of Hevea to a rubber orchard, requiring all the orchardist's skills. Important among these skills is the exacting craft of grafting: the placing together of two cut plant surfaces, as a rule from different plants, in a way that permits them to grow together. The area in which the graft is inserted is called the stock; the part inserted, the scion. Bud-grafting, or budding, works best with Hevea. This consists in cutting a bud or eye attached to a small piece of bark from a young branch of a high-yielding clonal tree and inserting it in a corresponding cut made in the stem of another plant. The "stock" is a healthy seedling tree, including a vigorous root system, and it will presently be transferred from the nursery to the open field. The bud-grafter carefully cleans the lower six inches of the stock, then makes a vertical cut about two and a half inches long through the entire bark structure. Next he makes a parallel cut about three-quarters of an inch from the first and to within an inch of the "shoulder" or ground terminal of the stock. He joins the parallel gashes with a horizontal cut, permits the latex to run, and wipes away the white coagulum.

Then he takes his budwood, locates a suitable bud and, using an extremely sharp knife, removes the bud with a chip of underlying wood attached. He painstakingly peels the bark from the accompanying bit of wood, and so shapes a "bud patch," preferably about two inches long. This he carefully inserts into the stock wound; then binds the bud patch, first with a fine string or a raffia fiber (taken from the piassava palm); covers the wound with a spiraled binding of waterproof tape, and seals the top of the tape bandage with waterproof wax.

In Liberia the most favorable budding season is between March and August, preferably on rainless days, which at this time of the year are not conveniently frequent. The budwood is cut, usually on the day it is used, from nursery stock, and bud-grafted on healthy seedling trees about nine months old. If the treatment is successful, the bud becomes an integral part of the stock, which within a year or less is ready to be planted in the grove.

The introduction of new clones of Hevea emphasized disease problems and disease-control practices. Like all other crops, rubber trees suffer from a number of diseases, though for the most part Hevea diseases are caused by fungi which attack root, stem, trunk, or leaf, singly or in combination. Particularly in the case of young trees, the root rots are the most serious and the hardest to detect. White root rot *(Fomes lignosus)* and brown root rot *(Fomes noxius)* are the two most serious of the root diseases. Both result from underground fungous spores, which germinate on the host roots and secrete poisonous enzymes in the root tissues. As the infection spreads, the tree's foliage begins to wilt; the leaves turn yellow and presently die. The only control measure is to identify the infected trees promptly, dig them out, and burn the infected roots.

Dry rot *(Ustulina zonata)* is another insidious fungus that attacks exposed wounds on the trunk or stem of the tree, usually the lower part of the trunk. The best preventive is to take every precaution to avoid making bark wounds, and to paint the unavoidable wounds with a suitable disinfectant. "Die back" is a term for the severe diseases that bring about a progressive withering of the tender young shoots. It is caused by at least four different fungi, all spread by wind-blown spores. The treatment consists in pruning away the infected plants and burning all discarded material. Significantly, a healthy tree is usually able to throw off the malady.

"Pink disease," a stem malady caused by another fungus *(Corticium salmonicolor)*, is a common enemy to many types of tropical vegetation including rubber trees. On these it usually appears as a white or pink incrustation of mycelium, usually at the forks of the branches. The only remedy known at present is vigilance: frequent inspection of all trees, removal of the early incrustations, burning the spores and painting the scraped areas with coal tar or other disinfectants, and pruning off and promptly burning all diseased branches.

"Black thread," a disease of the tapping panel of the bearing trees, is perhaps the most serious of the fungous pests. It is apparently spread by tiny spores carried by the wind or rain or sometimes on the blades of tapping knives. Fine black lines first appear on the bark just above the tapping cut. Presently these lines fuse and form cankerous areas; then the latex cells begin to rupture, and swollen calluses and bark wounds result. Preventive measures are imperative if the tree is to remain in bearing. Throughout the wet season the tapper smears each tapping cut with a mixture of palm oil and fungicide, and carefully dresses each of the tree's wounds with the sterilizing mixture.

Another perennial enemy of Hevea trees is the destroyer called brown bast – actually a physiological degeneration of the latex-yielding system which results from too rapid harvest of the liquid rubber, and more particularly from the too rapid loss of bark in the progress of tapping. Some clones and individual trees are more subject to brown bast than others, though no Hevea tree yet known is entirely immune. The symptoms are maddeningly deliberate. The latex begins to flow feebly. The surrounding bark areas become swollen and discolored. Peculiar swells and ridges appear in the bark, and in extreme cases the tree ceases to bear latex. Defensive action stresses the planting of clones or selected trees with the strongest resistance to the degeneration; the reduction of tapping schedules that tend to consume the vital bark more rapidly than the tree can replace it; and the prompt removal of all young trees that seem predisposed to the condition. Invariably, losses from brown bast rise sharply during or after periods of particularly heavy tapping.

The diseases here mentioned are more or less common in all rubber-growing lands. Figuratively, they are the colds, mumps, measles, pneumonia, even the cancer of the Hevea family. Fortunately, Liberian rubber has never suffered from the wicked South American "leaf disease": a windblown, round-spore fungus that blackens and kills the Hevea leaves and thus weakens, stunts, and eventually destroys the tree. Fortunately, too, the introduction of higher-yielding clonal rubber has not seriously raised the toll of disease loss. But the latter is due to no lucky happenchance.

From their beginning the new groves of clonal Hevea have been laboratories and proving grounds for combating the many fungous enemies which if unopposed could very well destroy the source of natural rubber. Decided progress is being made in breeding rubber trees along specific lines of disease resistance.

Nevertheless, in Liberia the rubber-tapper does double duty as a tree doctor. In addition the Firestone plantations maintain expertly trained "disease gangs," who regularly visit and inspect every tree. They report all appearances of fungi and seek to remedy them. In cases where there are no known remedies, the disease gang fells the sick tree, digs out its roots, records and takes samples of the fungus for delivery to the research pathologists, and then burns the evidence.

All in all, the successful introduction of clonal Hevea has been among the most significant current developments in all the world-benefiting fields of tropical agriculture and forestry. The little-known story of the upbreeding of Hevea trees indicates various possibilities for making the agrarian tropics far more beneficial to all peoples than they have ever been before.

Liberia continues to serve as the proving ground for an experiment that has vast and hopeful implications for all the tropics and many farming lands as well. In terms of creative research, the scientific staffs of the one-time great experiment stations of Sumatra, Java, and Malaya have been the greatest single benefactors of Hevea. But in terms of the actual and current propagation of high-yielding clonal rubber, Liberia now leads the tropical world. Rubber growers in Liberia now carry on from the point where the great Dutch and British naturalists were obliged, because of the Japanese invasion, to abandon their memorable work.

This has given Liberia a distinguished advantage over all other centers of natural rubber. At the time of Pearl Harbor barely one-tenth of Far East Hevea rubber then in harvest was from improved clones. The rest was from seedling trees with average yields per acre rarely exceeding 400 pounds yearly — roughly a third of the potential yield in Liberia.

Liberia's rubber lands have come into bearing with at least two-thirds of their total acreage planted to improved, yielding clones. The overall average yield of Liberia today, including seedling trees and the preponderant majority of young trees, is around 800 pounds of dry rubber per acre yearly. Thousands of acres of the older clonal rubber are scoring average yields in excess of 1,200 pounds per acre yearly; a few in excess of 1,400. This may well be symbolic of a new age of greater abundance in the potentially bountiful tropics. It is unquestionable proof of Liberia's sound position in the international agronomy of natural rubber, which can be even more important during the years immediately ahead than it has been during the years just past.

Chapter Seven

Firestone in Liberia

THE MIGRATION of crops, like the migration of peoples, combines social and economic history. Inevitably the beginning of a new crop is a far-reaching social phenomenon as well as an agricultural and an economic milestone. A crop begins to be born when someone identifies in the wilds a particular plant or family of plants that shows promise of some particular usefulness.

The chosen wild plant may thrive in the nursery or field or garden. More frequently it does not. If the transfer from the wilds to cultivated land is successful, the specimen in question is still then merely an economic plant. It becomes a crop only after a number of people have succeeded in growing and using it over a considerable period of time.

That statement is vague, but in general it is valid. Practically speaking, the valuable and durable crop must have been reborn into the domain of public use.

Usually any plant that people elect to change to a crop shows considerable mutation during its period of transition from the wilds to domestic cultivation. There are varied and often subtle changes in the flowering, seeding, and growth sequences of the plant. Usually, too, the plant hunter begins the process of selective breeding the moment he chooses a wild plant and transfers it to his garden. The particular type of soil and climate into which the wild plant is moved, the prevalent techniques of cultivation, harvest, and replanting, and the varying needs and the living standards of the transplanter also influence the transformation. It is usually decades or generations later when the chosen weed, bush, vine, or tree finally emerges as a valuable crop.

Thus every crop is a social document as well as a notable economic force: a document conceived and written by the curiosity, enterprise, planning, toil and sweat, sometimes the blood, of real people. For these there is often compensation. Once established, a single crop can, and repeatedly does, sustain millions or even hundreds of millions of people. Rice and corn — which taken together supply the primary subsistence for about two-thirds of the world's population — are impressive examples. So is the white potato, that edible tuber from the Andes that has become a basic food of Central and Western Europe; so are barley and wheat, which have helped decisively in shaping the maps of at least half the earth.

Cotton, tobacco, corn, and wheat, separately or collectively, have written a great part of American history. Sugar cane, the Hevea rubber tree, the banana, coconut, oil palms, bamboo, and such fiber sources as abacá, piassava, or sisal are among the tropical and subtropical plants which after establishment as principal crops have done most not only to found tropical nations but also to initiate a great number of international industries that affect all of us.

As the story of natural rubber proves particularly well, crops are also social institutions. They rarely remain confined to a single country. Inevitably one man's field or pasture or grove becomes part of the economic balance and body politic of his community or nation. Individual crops survive and multiply by virtue of man's enterprise, work, risk, and planning. But inevitably, if they survive and multiply they must somehow become coördinated with other crops that are also part of the economic and social structure of the area, or nation, or continent. New crops must be coördinated with crops already established. And they must fill a role in the lives and the times of the people who grow them.

The introduction of the Hevea tree as the source of a principal crop is more than usually difficult, because Hevea requires perennial forestry. The tree *Hevea brasiliensis* is one of at least 16,000 varieties of "higher plants" that are indigenous to the vast Amazon Basin. Liberia, covering about 45,000 of the almost 12,000,000 square miles of Africa, is the home of perhaps 1,600,000 of Africa's estimated 150 million people. Thus Hevea came to Africa as a minor crop for a small area of a vast continent. This fact may also indicate a pattern for crop introduction in the future.

Certainly the introduction of rubber into Liberia offers a heartening story of Americans and Africans working together. Logically enough, the chronicle began with exploration. A Firestone location party traveled down the seacoast and probed inland up the many rivers. Donald A. Ross, an old-line British rubber planter long experienced in Malaya, recognized the rolling hills and deep-soiled valleys as potential sites for rubber plantations. At that time (1924) there was only one small Hevea rubber estate in all Liberia — a British-founded property called Mount Barclay, which is located about twenty miles inland and upcoast from Monrovia. The original proprietors had abandoned the estate, and during the intervening years the groves of rubber trees had grown up in bush.

But Mount Barclay proved valuable in at least two respects. It proved beyond possibility of question that Hevea trees thrive in Liberia, and it served as a valuable pilot plant for the much larger Firestone operations which were launched a short distance beyond it. Firestone leased Mount Barclay and returned it to rubber production.

Harvey S. Firestone, Jr., who had selected Liberia and completed the negotiations in connection with the planting agreement, took over the general management of the rubber-growing enterprise. Among the then youthful Firestone pioneers in Liberia were William D. Hines, a young newspaper man from Pennsylvania, Ohio, Paris, and intermediate points, who dealt with the Liberian Government; Ross Wilson, a youthful six-foot-plus football-playing engineer from Akron; Bert Vipond, a young Pennsylvanian with a degree in agriculture from Penn State; Dean Ashley, Warren Brockett, Paul Dusenberry, Henry Heilman, and Frederick Helm. These and about thirty other young men from the States, most of them in their early twenties, were pioneering in answer to the usual need of jobs, the lure of tropical spaces, and eagerness to be on the ground floor of a new and different American enterprise. Whether or not they had come specifically in the quest of adventure, all of them overtook plenty of it.

No two tropical countries are precisely alike. The immediate challenge was to fit a big-scale tropical planting project into the economic and social needs of a nation which never before had a big-scale work project of any kind. One of the first drastic departures effected by Firestone was to introduce into Africa the American work day, a maximum of eight hours. Along with the almost Herculean task of clearing jungles, building roads, and developing plantation nurseries, the company also undertook to provide suitable housing, necessary medical services, weekly rice issues, and essential merchandising. It accepts the fact that the tropical employer's responsibilities for the welfare of his employees and their dependents cover all twenty-four hours of every day. Moreover, it sponsors suitable entertainment for the workers – preferably by enabling them to provide their own.

An important point is that the company makes use of native leadership. Just as the chief is essential to the tribe or town, so is the headman to the work party. He must be a natural-born leader and receive proper rewards and respect for his outstanding abilities. Workers require the right to select their own leaders, which they do by what to white men is a highly mysterious process of election. Once the headman is chosen, the workers follow him. If a worker is unable to get along with his headman, he is permitted to attach himself and his allegiance to another headman.

Working forces, usually twenty to thirty "boys," serve under their own selection of a headman. He in turn serves under an overseer or supervisor. The latter, according to native protocol, issues instructions or forwards criticism directly to the headman in charge, not to the individual worker. The integrity and the sanctity of the worker's person must at all times be respected. If a headman, overseer, or any other employee strikes, reprimands, or accuses a worker, the latter has recourse to a palaver hearing or other lawful representation.

From Akron, Ohio, Harvey S. Firestone spoke of Firestone labor policy in Liberia:

> ". . . This labor comes to us direct from its villages, often three or four hundred miles away, to take part for the first time in a large operation. Our recruiting has been evenly distributed over the country in order that no one section might suffer by sending us too many men at one time.
>
> "When an agent has assembled a group of natives – let us say about two hundred – they start for the plantations accompanied by an agent or messenger of their head

chief, who goes along to oversee their welfare. This trip through a long forest trail is a great adventure. Many of the men never traveled so far from home before. . . . Instead of living in coolie lines as laborers are commonly housed in the Far East, they build their own houses in their own way, setting up a new village in place of those left behind. These houses are built of poles with thatched roofs and the sides are covered with clay. . . .

"After the people have built their houses and arranged their villages, they are put to work felling and burning the forest or planting rubber trees in the territory already cleared. They work [no more than] eight hours a day. . . . So far as I know, we are the only employers of African labor to establish the American working day. . . ."

The practices in recruiting workers still remain substantially the same.

As the young rubber planters met the tribesmen of Liberia at first hand, they learned more about tribal differences in temperament and talents for work. For example, the Bassa people are a populous tribe, good-natured, hospitable, exceptionally talented in making and keeping homes, and without any particular prejudices against specific types of work including domestic service. The Belle people are superior farmers and builders; the Krus excel as boatmen, rivermen, and fishermen; the Mende have unique talents as policemen; the Grebos make superior farmers and mechanics; the Mandingos are the natural-born traders of the land; the Buzzies are highly talented workers with aptitudes for nursing and various technical pursuits. The newcomers observed that members of one tribe habitually prefer to roam about, while those of another are inclined to stay at home.

Fitting the new rubber-planting enterprise into the old and proved patterns of life and work of West Africa involved planning and building tribe-style huts, villages, and towns for the rubber-plantation workers. It called for the adoption of African work traditions. For example, forest or bush felling is a prerequisite to planting rubber or any other frontier crop. Long lines of axmen must work in rhythm to the beating of drums and the chanting of singers. In that manner the work goes forward. Otherwise it lags.

The myriad tasks of planting rubber groves led to the discovery of numerous and often subtle rivalries among the various tribes. If a Bassa boy should hesitate or consider himself unable to lift a log or place a stone, the suggestion that a Buzzie could easily do the chore will almost invariably induce the Bassa to lift the log or place the stone with the greatest of ease.

Yet the distinct awareness of tribal identity rarely hinders workers from different tribes in working together or playing together, or living in the same village, or otherwise remaining friends. Frequently a headman succeeds in leading a work crew with members from several different tribes. The rural Liberians, to whom tribe means nation, show a marked talent for internationalism.

As the Firestone men discovered, the feat of supplying and organizing a plantation labor force is an excellent practical example of internationalism. During a typical month (in this instance, October 1946) the labor population employed by the Firestone plantations included the following tribesmen in a total plantation working force of approximately 30,000:

Bassa	2,685
Belle	345
Buzzie	4,004
Chien	31
Dey	73
Gbandi	1,594

Tribe	Number
Gio	3,975
Gizzie	1,969
Gola	766
Grebo	2,585
Kpelle	5,486
Kran	571
Kru	563
Mandingo	247
Mano	3,666
Mendi	1,197
Vai	259
TOTAL	30,016

In backcountry Liberia a prospective employer who wants to get workers does not post notices or print advertisements or telephone to employment agencies. Instead, he applies by the process of informal palaver to a chief – either a clan chief or a paramount chief – and as a rule receives and gives in kind a suitable "dash." The labor seeker states the wage and other employment terms. The chief accepts or declines. If he accepts, he specifies the number of his tribesmen who may work and suggests the length of their employment. In many instances he stipulates that his tribe members must return to the tribal lands and help in clearing land, building roads, or other tribal work during the next dry season. The chief then names the particular members of his tribe or village who will work on the plantation. The transaction of hiring is supervised by a district commissioner as representative of the Liberian government. The tribe member who accepts or is assigned employment is expected by his chief to send back to the tribe some part of his earnings, preferably in useful merchandise. Most, though not invariably all, of the tribesmen nominated to work "by the rubber" actually report at the plantations. Here is a typical recruiting report ("CC" being Clan Chief, and "PC" Paramount Chief):

Chief	District	Section	Tribe	No. of Boys Sent	No. of Boys Arr'd
CC Kpama Yomo	Kakata	Kpama	Kpelle	15	15
CC Kpabah Gbeles	"	Gbelee To	"	10	7
CC Gbalokai	"	Konoyea	"	11	11
CC K. Daniel	"	Queline	"	14	10
CC K. Lupu	"	Menkellie	"	14	14
CC D. Livingstone	"	Sanoyea	"	10	8
CC Kpenbah	"	Gbama	"	11	11
PC B. Zinnah	Bopolu-Suehn	Bopolu	"	24	24
PC Menyongai	Kakata	Gibi	Bassa	42	38
PC Vana Woo	Bopolu-Suehn	Kongba	Gola	13	13
PC Varfee Sirleaf	"	Mecca	Mandingo	9	9
PC Mongru	Saniquellie	Gborplay	Geh	32	32
PC Mongru	"	Stolay	"	21	21
PC Wydordea	Tappita	Messonah	Mano	27	21
PC G. Toweh	"	Boe-Queela	Gio	18	8
PC Wydordea	"	Yarwin	Mano	17	12
PC Weipah Paye	"	Doe	Gio	16	11
CC Segbeh Dahn	"	Gbai-Gblor	"	14	6
PC Nyonton Paye	"	Kpiaplay	Krahn	16	16
			Total	334	287

Inevitably, "bush trips" into the interior are prerequisite to the mustering of labor. Diaries or journals of these bush trips still provide some of the most revealing commentaries on the still magnificent jungle frontier. H. H. Burgess, of Firestone plantations staff, reported:

"I spent eight days at the Zorzor mission, resting, visiting and collecting jigger fleas in my feet. . . . I rode to Fissibui, following up some rumored leopard skins. . . . All along the trails the Buzzies were busy felling and cleaning rice farms. Buzzies who had formerly worked on the rubber divisions stopped me to say 'Plenty Howdo!' The horsebacked white man attracts attention, and the native telegraph system works fast even in rice fields.

"I rode Chief Bonaco's horse to Kpayia, then sent the horse back and attempted to cross the St. Paul River.

However, this well-marked crossing (on the map) did not exist, so we returned and trekked upstream to wade a tributary of the St. Paul near Wengue into French Guinea. . . . We rafted the Nimba (St. Paul) and found to our surprise that the raftsmen expect no dash. It is part of the Government road system.

"The sky was cloudy and the road clear, so we hurried up to make up for the time lost the previous day in crossing the border. From Bomakoma . . . we asked for accommodations. The chief was on his farm, so no one moved. We started to move on as the speechless chief arrived. He spread his arms to gesture 'You cannot go.' He turned, collared a loiterer, and marched him to the rest house to clean our hut. He brought us a chicken, some pineapple, and some cooking pots, and sent his women scurrying for hot water and chicken eggs. I slept comfortably on a mud bed, and after dashing the hospitable chief a pair of socks and a piece of fudge hurried away at dawn for another thirty-mile hike.

"We came into the Mendingo town of Takpse where chanting men, overly clothed women, braying jackasses, long-legged sheep, and a continuous line of cola-laden natives crossing the Liberian boundary told the occupation of the town, which is trading. Next morning we moved on to Gamu, Yvala, and crossed the St. John River on a pontoon bridge. In the shade of a roadside hut I sucked lustily on a juicy pineapple, because as we neared civilization my boy as usual had neglected to boil sufficient water. . . ."

As the planters also learned, most tribespeople are remarkably gregarious. They prefer not to live alone and, if required to do so, they definitely do not like it. When a worker is assigned his hut he invites a friend, usually three or four friends, to come and live with him. Therefore, huts designed for one or at most two or three occupants may become packed with as many as ten or twelve.

The tribesman has many other recurring characteristics.

His neck and arms are, as a rule, remarkably strong, and when first introduced to a white man's tool he is likely to break it — simply because he has never before measured his brawn on the alien implements.

The Liberian worker is rarely excessively fat or excessively lean. He seldom runs, usually walks slowly, and works rhythmically. As a rule his leg muscles are not nearly so well developed as those of his arms and neck. Often he is ambidextrous. Not infrequently, his eyesight is subnormal as compared with the white man's averages, but his hearing and his sense of smell are superior, as are his capacities for "feeling" the probability of storm, the proximity of predatory animals, or other dangers. He acquires his skills early; the years between fourteen and seventeen are usually the most effective learning years.

The work of pioneering rubber-plantings in Liberia was enormously difficult. But from the beginning it was an immensely revealing adventure. The rubber-planting frontiersmen traveled among the tribes, worked with and among the native peoples, and in the beginning lived much as the tribesmen lived. At times they saw and heard hungry leopards prowling close beside the hut doors or compound gates. With tens of thousands of acres to be cleared and planted to Hevea trees, there was not time at first for building enough roads or houses. So the young men tramped the jungle trails, ate the jungle fare, and lived in the thatch-roofed huts, taking considerable chances with mosquitoes, prowling boa constrictors, and the more deadly, though less visible, microörganisms of disease. Sickness, particularly malaria and dysentery, was frequent enough, but there were no deaths.

They worked for months and years with little sight or company of their kind. Three of the early planters of the far downshore Cavally plantations formed a covenant by which each agreed that on every third Sunday he would tramp through the bush the requisite distance – somewhere between eight and fifteen miles – to visit the other two. Thus they were able to come together once a week. Otherwise they lived and worked as the tribesmen did.

One of the same three veterans tells a story of the early days in the Harbel bush. He recalls how four of the palefaces came together one evening in a raffia-thatched mud hut, played cards and ate dinner from a homemade pole table, and in due time began telling snake stories.

For hours they swapped yarns about the murderous green mamba snakes and the huge boa constrictors that each had either killed or succeeded in avoiding. They told of snakes that take shelter in native huts during daylight hours, hide upon the dusty rafter poles, and at nighttime spring down among sleeping occupants.

The horror fest was gradually approaching its climax when down from a rafter pole fell a green mamba, small but deadly poisonous, squarely on the table. As one man, the four yarn-swappers leaped high into the air and charged madly through the thatched walls of the hut. Next morning the hut was abandoned. But the four man-high holes in its palm-thatched walls remained.

By 1928, when Britain's Stevenson Plan was beginning to fall apart and Holland's big lush island colony of Sumatra was about to take over the balance of power in natural-rubber production, the Firestone plantations had assumed at least a semblance of real plantations. On the rolling hill lands beyond the Du and the Farmington rivers inland from Monrovia, and in the far downcoast area at Cape Palmas near the Cavally River boundary of the French Ivory Coast, far-spreading cleared fields were replacing what had lately been dense and untenanted bush and jungle. By the millions and tens of millions, ground shrubs, vines, and giant trees of the great rain forest – some of the trees as tall as a medium skyscraper – had fallen to the stubby, hand-swung axes and cutlasses of tribesmen newly transformed into plantation workers. Part of the more valuable timber had been recovered for use in building commissaries, storages, and homes for employees. But of necessity most of the vast forest growth was being burned away by raging dry-season fires painstakingly started by the tribesmen who kept to traditional land-clearing and brush-burning practices. The dark-skinned wielders of axes and cutlasses piled the forest debris in drying windrows and then marched through the "burns" applying oversize torches. Smoke and flames rose high and far. Forest animals ran for life as the fire took over.

Then in the ash-littered, char-blackened earth, other workmen planted hundreds of thousands of young rubber trees, switchlike seedlings that were being raised in open nursery plots planted with Hevea seed imported from other West African areas. They aligned the rows with primitive surveying instruments, dug deep holes about fifteen feet apart in rows also about fifteen feet apart, and planted the slender seedling trees – some 190 to the acre. When the trees are about five years old they are "test-tapped." The weaker producers are removed, and the stands are then thinned occasionally to a permanent population of about 110 trees to the acre.

Firestone's initial planning and planting were based directly on the plantation practices and work sequences developed and proved in the great Hevea groves of Malaya, Sumatra, and other Far Eastern tropics. But numerous local adaptations were required. As the planters in Liberia discovered, Hevea, like most other international crops, varies considerably with the particular geographic area in which it is placed. Accordingly in many respects the planters from the United States were better off unimpeded by the obligations of an older planting tradition.

As the rounded, shiny, brown-splotched Hevea seeds sprouted in nursery beds of rich spaded soil, and as plantation workers transplanted the young seedlings to the newly burned fields, Liberian rubber-growing began to develop and prove modes and techniques of its own. But the overall pattern was laboriously specific: Clear the land; burn the bush; dig the holes; remove as many roots and as much debris as practical. Plant the seeds in raised beds at least a foot above the adjacent ground level; provide drainage; divide an acre of newly cleared land into fifteen or sixteen such nursery beds, leaving narrow pathways between them. Take the Hevea seeds (which are about the size of medium marbles), press them into the finely tilled soil with the grooved side down, and cover them with approximately an inch of fine damp sand or silt. Use the same tender care that you would use in planting a cherished vegetable garden. If the seeds do not germinate within two weeks, throw them away and plant others. As many as 38,000 infant trees can be started on a single acre of nursery clearing; this requires about 336 pounds of seeds.

As a rule the seedling trees are ready for field planting the second year after the seeds are "set." (If clonal rubber is to be planted, the young seedling trees may be bud-grafted in the nursery nine or ten months after the seeds are planted.)

"Bush-clearing"—felling the tropical wilds—remains one of the most energetic pursuits of man. Usually it begins when crews of ax men and cutlass-swingers enter a surveyed area and open direct attack on the smaller trees and bushes. The vines and trees of less than four inches' diameter must be cut off at ground level. When the underbrush is cleared the big trees can be felled, leaving stumps three or four feet high. Branches are chopped off the trunks. The felling ends when the entire area is piled knee-high or at times head-high with jungle debris.

The burning is best accomplished during February or March, the season of the drying harmattan winds. Hundreds, sometimes thousands, of acres of land are cleared by a single fire. Armed with bamboo torches and warily watching for wind direction, the workmen systematically set the fire. Without great caution and skill the feat would be an open flirtation with death and destruction; but the Liberian tribesman handles fire with an almost uncanny skill. The burners line up facing the wind, each man standing about thirty feet from the man next to him, each bearing a long-handled torch. Then the workers move slowly forward into the wind. Each lights his torch and applies fire as he proceeds. In the tropics as elsewhere, fire is the supreme cleanser.

Then come the processes of "lining" and "holing." The holes are three feet deep and about two feet in diameter at the bottom and three at the top. After the holes are dug they are filled with surface soil, which is permitted to become settled and compact under a succession of rains. Then a deep hole is punched with a "dibble" stick. In it the tap root is inserted. When planting is done well, an average of ninety percent of the young trees survive.

After the nursery trees are planted in the groves, the land is planted to a cover crop that conserves the soil. In Liberia the creeping leguminous plant Pueraria *(Javanica)*, another valuable Javanese import, has proved to be best for this purpose. Meanwhile, every young rubber tree is circled by a four-foot ring of cleared earth, a process called "ring weeding." Then as the young trees grow, the pueraria vine is permitted to touch the base of the trees.

Ordinarily tapping begins as soon as the trunk diameter of the young tree reaches five inches at waist height.

The trees are carefully counted, mapped, and numbered, and all that are malformed, injured, diseased, or stunted are destroyed. The approved trees are then counted off in "tasks" of from 250 to 300 trees, which in time constitute the daily work assignment of one full-time tapper.

Technical details begin to crowd in closely as soon as a rubber grove approaches the point of harvest. The factors of chemistry and bacteriology are particularly impressive. One begins to appreciate this when he undertakes to compute the daily harvests of milky latex in pounds, tons, or bales of dry rubber. As a year-'round average, about one-third of the initial weight of the freshly harvested latex becomes dry rubber or its equivalent. That is, the routine coagulation of 1,000 pounds of average latex (of which about 36 percent is total solids) provides approximately 330 pounds of dry rubber. On Firestone plantations the greater part of the best-quality liquid latex is put through power-operated centrifuges (oversize and extra heavy cream separators) immediately after harvest. From the average 1,000 pounds of fresh latex (accurately harvested and treated with a suitable anticoagulant) comes about 476 pounds of liquid-rubber concentrate, which has a dry-rubber content of approximately 60 percent and is the most valuable natural rubber now on the market. It is sold, on the basis of total solid-rubber content, at a substantial premium over ordinary crêpe or sheet rubber, the preponderant market type of natural rubber.

The same thousand pounds of fresh latex that yields an average of 476 pounds of centrifuged concentrate also yields approximately 524 pounds of "skim," which has an average of twelve percent total solids and a dry-rubber content of about 8.4 percent. When coagulated, the residue of skim provides about 44 pounds of crêpe rubber, which is pressed into bales, each weighing 224 pounds or one-tenth of a long ton, which is still the traditional measure for rubber.

But what rubber plantation records term "total crop" includes a great deal besides concentrate and crêpe. Usually, of all recoverable rubber produced on a well-managed plantation approximately one-third of tree latex can be centrifuged to make concentrate, while about 48 percent is liquid latex which can, by methodical coagulation and drying, be converted to compact bales of crêpe rubber. The rest of the crop is harvested as solid or coagulated rubber of various grades, such as "cup lump," "tree lace," "bark scrap," etc. But all the crop has uses and value.

The procedures of rubber harvest remain in continuing mutation. Practical, untiring study and research are indispensable. As a rule, rubber production climbs with the coming of the dry season when weather conditions are most nearly ideal for the harvest. But this rule is not absolute, since the annual rainfall of Liberia varies markedly from place to place. (For Liberia as a whole, the average annual rainfall is probably somewhere near 106 inches annually; for most of the rubber-producing areas, from 145 to 160 inches a year.)

Rainfall is enormously important to the rubber farmer since its usual seasonal variations pose many critical problems. The new groves of Hevea must be planted and new houses must be built during the months with comparatively low rainfall—that is, between mid-November and mid-April. And though the harvest is year-'round, as a rule the heaviest yields of latex must be recovered during these same dry months.

For the extremely wet season drainage is essential, and the dry season can raise serious problems in water supply. An adequate year-'round water supply is one of the serious problems that confront Liberia, and indeed West Africa as a whole. Surface wells, still the principal water source for most Liberians (and other Africans), overflow during the wet seasons, yet too often vanish in the dry seasons. Time and again entire tribes have been obliged to move because the water supply failed. In Liberian towns drinking water must still be bought from peddlers or well-owners during times of drought. Thus, even in heavy rainfall country, the need for more and bigger water pipelines and reservoirs keeps growing.

More and more clearly, too, the modern Hevea plantation becomes an extensive chemistry laboratory. The premium grades of natural rubber are made from tree latex processed into a stable-liquid form. Preserving the latex this way requires the use of chemicals to retard the growth of the particular bacteria that cause coagulation of the latex. The most common anticoagulants are ammonia and sodium sulphite. If the latex is to be processed through centrifugal machines, it must be treated with ammonia immediately on being harvested. Latex for conversion to sheet rubber is usually treated with sodium sulphite preparatory to plantation processing.

Thus the tapper carries a diluted solution of anticoagulant to his task and places a few drops of it in the cups at the time he taps the trees. After he has carried the latex from the grove to the collection station, additional anticoagulant is added. Practically speaking, the basic chemistry of natural rubber requires the use of anticoagulants both in the field and at the stations, and of a highly active coagulant at the processing factory. Formic acid is one of the most commonly used coagulants.

Bacteriology is likewise an inescapable part of the natural-rubber game. It necessitates standards of cleanliness as exacting as those of a well-run modern dairy. For in addition to the complex hydrocarbons of rubber, the latex of the Hevea tree contains numerous nonrubber solids—proteins, soaps, esters, sterols, enzymes, sugars, etc.—and is an ideal host for bacterial life. Every minute the latex stands, growth and change take place in its bacterial population. The acid content increases rapidly with the multiplication of bacteria, and even with the most rigid sanitary precautions the latex is far from sterile. Thus a rubber plantation remains an extensive arena for bacteriological transformations.

As a rule the bacteria that cause obnoxious odors are resistant to ammonia and multiply rapidly in all or any residues of latex that are permitted to remain in hose, tanks, or other containers. Cleanliness is essential, therefore, throughout all the steps in collecting and processing the latex. The receptacles must be kept immaculate, and collection stations and processing plants must remain in a perpetual state of housecleaning. The life of the rubber producer is also one of suds, scrubbing, and sniffing, as well as patient handicraft, muscle power, and engine power.

Around the clock and the calendar thousands of competent tappers must cause the trees to "bleed" latex and see the latex delivered at the collection stations. There clerks and chemists weigh and record it, treat it and store it for the daily rounds of the big tank trucks which carry the latex (by 1400-gallon or 1800-gallon trailer loads) to the central plantation processing factory. Here, pipelines move the latex from a central receiving tank to the power-driven centrifuges and to the portable coagulation vats. The latter feed into formidable lines of power-operated mangles, washing machines, and beaters which, with a great deal of energetic human assistance, process the rubber. Automatic conveyors forward it to be hung in long, thin sheets in the big, temperature-controlled infernos of the drying rooms. From there the bright amber sheets of rubber are graded and carried to the hydraulic baling machines, which compress them into standard-size bales of 224 pounds each. Other workmen then dust these with soapstone label and number them, and otherwise make them ready for shipment and ultimate factory lines.

The harvest of natural rubber is one of the most exacting and laborious of all agricultural industries. It is a unique blending of town and country life, of handicraft, power machinery, public utility, and incessant motion of hands and wheels. Technically, Liberia's enterprise of natural rubber is by far the most advanced in the world today. Though some of its facilities are local adaptations of those of older and bigger producing centers, at least as many are entirely original. The final test of success or failure in rubber production is, of course, the practical proof of the industrial utility of the product. Liberian rubber has endured and fulfilled the more and more exacting demands of industry. As the growing and processing of rubber become part of the primary economy and social structure of Liberia, the sheer contrast between the technologies of one of the most complex of world industries and the primitive integrity of the black-green African frontier grows even more conspicuous.

Chapter Eight

Hevea and Liberia

BY THE MIDDLE 1930s Hevea rubber had become a major resource of Liberia without violating her national sovereignty and without devitalizing her tribes. On the whole, the introduction of Hevea rubber into Liberia has proved more successful than most other international adventures in crop introduction.

Yet its problems and needs and challenges keep growing. Rubber remains a changing crop on a persisting tropical frontier. It is a full-time-employment crop which requires about twenty times as many man-hours per acre as corn, the foremost crop of the United States. Even so, only about three percent of Liberia's people work regularly for wages.

The status of rubber-plantation ownership is also exceptional. Firestone owns no land in Liberia. The lands worked by the American company are actually leased from the Liberian government at annual rentals ranging from six cents an acre (land may be bought outright by any Liberian citizen at prices averaging as low as 50 cents an acre) to several dollars an acre. By the terms of Liberia's constitution only citizens of the Republic may own land within Liberia, and citizenship in turn, though including all the tribal peoples, remains limited to persons of African descent.

Of the approximately 25 million acres of Liberian land, only about half of one percent is regularly planted to crops. Today about half of all Liberia's cultivated land is planted to rubber, which in terms of exports and revenues is the heavily preponderant crop. For example, in 1925, before rubber had become established, Liberian export trade totaled $1,911,000, and the total government revenues were $591,420. At the close of the 1945 fiscal year the Government's income totaled $2,041,999, and exports totaled $12,-373,491 of which $11,614,131 was rubber. Significantly, during the period of transition to rubber the condition of Liberian treasury changed from virtual default to outstanding solvency, while the remaining national debt declined to only slightly more than 50 cents per capita, which is apparently the lowest in any sovereign nation in the world today.

Obviously rubber cannot be the entire story of Liberia but, as living history proves, it is essential to good lives for Liberians. The crux of that proof emerged from the tempests and the maelstroms of World War II.

Mankind has found many ways of naming that war, only a few of them compatible with the proprieties of book-publishing. Whatever else it may have been, World War II was certainly a vast sequence of collisions and social revolutions born of the tragic segregation of goods and ideologies. As equilibrium vanished, social, economic, and political structures began to tumble like big trees in the swath of a tornado. Falling trees, so to speak, crashed down on still greater numbers of smaller trees that might otherwise have escaped the wrath of the storm. Many tropical countries and colonies were among these little trees that were storm-toppled. Tropical countries are preponderantly agrarian, and the great majority of all tropical peoples are farmers of one sort or another. The producing earth writes the greater part of tropical history.

Offsetting the usual advantages of longer growing seasons, low tax structures, cheaper lands, and what should be (though often are not) generally favorable environments for people, is the truth that tropical products are almost invariably at the mercy of a buyer's market. Chronically lacking in industrial facilities and power sources, tropical economies usually rise slightly and fall drastically with the varying strength or weakness of temperate-zone industrial purchases. The absence of balance among the major industrial nations during the quarter-century between the outbreak of World War I and that of World War II reacted directly and in substantial part direly throughout the tropical world.

For the United States, Pearl Harbor was the lightning flash that revealed the alarming inconsistencies in the established sources of the many tropical harvests which we are obliged to import in either war or peace. As one conspicuous instance, during 1941 the United States imported about 866,000 long tons of natural rubber, the greater part of it for routine peacetime uses. About 97 percent of all that immense load of natural rubber had come from a relatively tiny area: considerably less than 9,000,000 acres of Hevea plantings in the hot Pacific lands – for the most part in the Malayan Peninsula and the big mackerel-shaped island of Sumatra. Thus the great tree crop born in the Amazon Basin had grown to be the least protectable of the great American imports.

Since 1912 natural rubber had remained our foremost import from the tropics. But as of 1941 natural rubber was only the largest of a long list of tropical commodities whose major production had become segregated in relatively tiny spheres of the Far Pacific lands.

Year after year the U. S. Department of Commerce statistics had recorded our extreme and dangerous favoritism towards the exports from developed colonies of the South Pacific and our habitual slipshod neglect of such great tropical reservoirs as Africa and South America. During 1938, for example, United States commercial firms had imported $11,401,000 worth of coconut oil from Ceylon and the Netherlands Indies, and only a few hundred dollars' worth from all the other palm-bearing tropics. Our purchases of tropical fibers totaled $20,228,000, of which 76 percent was supplied from a few hundred square miles of Pacific islands. All in all, during the final year of comparative peace the United States purchased about 91 percent of all imports of tropical crops from the Netherlands Indies, Malaya, Ceylon, Burma, and Indo-China; less than 2 percent from Africa, and less than 5 percent from all the American tropics—this despite the fact that shipping distances from United States ports and airports to major ports of the African or the American tropics average considerably less than one-third of those from the Far Pacific.

As almost every schoolchild now knows, the greatest and most damaging of all wars proved the appalling danger of such concentration. Within one hundred days after Pearl Harbor, Japanese forces had fanned out to seize almost two and one-half million square miles of the Pacific tropics. The Eastern strongholds of natural rubber fell like card castles. Within three months their precious rubber supplies were cut off from us; their harbors were completely blocked; their shipping lanes were cut to pieces; their merchant shipping was sunk or dissipated over sea lanes that no navy or combination of navies could conceivably defend. Within one hundred days after Pearl Harbor the source of roughly nine-tenths of all our tropical imports, including many goods essential to winning a war, were in enemy hands.

By the end of 1942 – blackest of all the war years – the tragic hazards incident to segregation of the main sources of essential tropical goods were becoming tragic realities.

Adding irony to tragedy was the fact that Britain, France, and Holland, the three empires that had been permitted to dominate the sources of many tropical supplies for the particular advantage of a favored few of their citizens, were now bereft of those supplies and abjectly dependent on depleted American stores of critical staples that can be produced only in the tropics.

As the number-one warring power and preponderant supplier of the United Nations, the United States set about finding or establishing new sources of essential tropical commodities. The Defense Supplies Corporation, the Rubber Development Corporation, the Department of Agriculture, the War and Navy Departments, and many other arms and branches of the U. S. Government began a far-reaching, costly, and rather frantic quest to replace part of the tropical resources that had been lost to Japan.

Agencies of the U. S. Government undertook the procurement of wild rubber in 19 tropical countries; and promptly issued contracts for planting a total of approximately 50,000 acres of "lost crops" in the American tropics from Brazil to Mexico; such crops as Philippine abacá (the source of Manila rope for ship and plane operations); Malayan rotenone (a modern insecticide and delousing agent); roselle, a jutelike fiber, formerly grown in India; various essential or tropical grass oils formerly produced in Java; coconut and other palm oils formerly produced in Ceylon and the Netherlands Indies; cork, teak, and other strategic tropical timbers; tung-oil trees and many other tropical crops that were temporarily lost to us. The frenzied dash for procuring random bits of natural rubber was quickly outdistanced by a brilliant move into the manufacture of synthetic rubbers.

Nevertheless, rubber and rubber substitutes remained

the most critical deficit. There was not time enough to plant extensive acreages of Hevea trees and bring them into bearing. This, in turn, spotlighted the reality that among all the United Nations, Ceylon and Liberia could offer the most valuable resources of ready-established Hevea rubber plantations. Promptly and completely all Liberian rubber "went to war" at ceiling prices established by the United States Government.

Double panel tapping, "200 percent intensity," was instituted during June 1942 as an urgent war measure. The average yield for the first year of intensive tapping, November 1 to the following October 31, was 703.5 pounds. During 1942-43 (when the war needs for rubber were at the climax of urgency) the yield rose to 999.7 pounds of dry-rubber equivalent to the acre. During the critical war years millions of Liberian rubber trees, like so many millions of human beings, were giving their all to win. The adjustment of rubber yields to critical war needs was entirely unprecedented. Under-age trees were soon to yield more than 1,000 pounds of rubber to the acre yearly (any rubber planter's dream of divine abundance). Favorable clones and individual trees were measured for yield representing 2,000 pounds or even 2,500 pounds to the acre. But the average yield of half a ton to the acre, as effected on tens of thousands of Liberian acres, clearly proved that, in Liberia, Hevea had gone to war.

During this earlier and darker period Liberian rubber yields were statistics of life or death for Allied fighting forces. Particularly during the two darkest years that followed Pearl Harbor, every pound of natural rubber was potentially or actually a life-saving commodity. Millions of tires for planes, trucks, tractors, and jeeps were essential to the success—even to the survival—of land and sea fighting forces. A blowout, or a puncture, or the inability to replace a tire could and too often did spell death for one or for several men, along with the loss of essential equipment. At that time American factories had not become able to produce anywhere near enough synthetic rubber to fill the tremendous demands of war. Synthetic rubber was "on its way"; but, judging from the bleak news bulletins of the times, so was the ultimate tragedy of Axis victory.

Meanwhile from the Allied war capital of Washington, D. C., Federal agencies were working valiantly and with variable success to salvage rubber and to effect the conservation of truck and auto tires already in use. American rubber factories were tremendously engrossed in war manufacture. Their direct shortage lay in their basic manufacturing material.

Meanwhile, also, Liberia and Ceylon had become the greatest producing strongholds of natural rubber available to the United States and our allies, and Firestone's plantations were the largest integrated Hevea properties in bearing anywhere in the world. They are being expanded at the rate of about 5,000 acres yearly. As during the war years, practice continues to prove that for the manufacture of large tires for heavy planes and trucks – tires whose use involves extreme heat, friction, and load – natural rubber is still superior to synthetic. The synthetic is improving. But so, too, is the natural.

By the date of Pearl Harbor, Liberia was producing roughly 27 million pounds of natural rubber a year, or more than twice the combined yield of all of the American tropics. By the close of the war the Liberian total had risen to about 45 million pounds yearly. It is still conspicuously upward bound. Harvey S. Firestone, Jr. remains president of Firestone Plantations Company. Byron H. Larabee, a young lawyer from Indiana, is executive vice-president.

During the war years several thousand tons of native rubber of various types were procured from the wilds of Central America, thanks in considerable part to the efforts of Central American personnel of Goodyear, United Fruit, and American Chicle, and to government workers from several Federal departments. The United States' wild-rubber recovery program so expensively instituted in the Amazon Basin yielded a grand total of about 53,700 long tons of rubber of unstaple quality during the war years. The cost to the American people was about $300 million – more than $2.60 a pound. The United States purchased the entire Liberian crop at ceiling prices fixed by the United States to average about 26 cents a pound during the entire war period.

The earth-spanning quest for natural rubber during the war, however, demonstrated a number of things. Among them is the certainty that the days of wild rubber are forever finished; and that the Hevea tree is the only practicable source of natural rubber. Ventures in developing cryptostegia, or Mexican rubber vine (actually indigenous to Madagascar), failed with substantial loss to American taxpayers. The dryland Mexican guayule bush, long publicized and never well proved as a source of rubber, likewise failed to produce effectively.

Castilla, or castilloa, the indigenous rubber tree of central and northern South America, likewise did not provide encouraging yields, and the recovery of rubber from lobelia vines of interior Africa and other tropical lands was still more futile. The greatest of wars proved beyond doubt that clonal Hevea, developed by painstaking and time-consuming processes of selective breeding, bud-grafting, and diligent field observation, is the one natural-rubber source with a clearly promising future.

As the war lengthened, the U. S. Rubber Development Corporation and associated agencies appealed for intensified tapping as a temporary expedient for producing more rubber from available trees. Intensive tapping means double panel tapping; that is, opening on the trunk of each producing Hevea tree a "high panel" or half spiral, high up on the trunk, in addition to the usual panel.

At the time such a severe harvest procedure had never been accepted by Hevea growers. The usual harvest routine —"100 percent tapping"— ordinarily requires that each bearing tree be "bled" daily, usually for 14 or 15 successive days. Then the tree is permitted to rest for the same length of time. In all cases the latex is removed from only one "panel" or bark incision. In double panel tapping —"200 percent intensity"— a tree is bled every day, alternating between the high and the low panel. The intensity of the double panel tapping can be varied. For example, a plantation or grove may be divided into three parts, with two parts alternately in tapping and the third resting. This is called ABC tapping — or "133 percent intensity." The ABCD formula for "150 percent intensity" consists in dividing the grove into four parts and alternately tapping three and resting one; or tapping the high panels of two sections while resting the low panel of the others.

The general run of experienced rubber growers viewed double panel tapping with complete distrust. Any Hevea grower knows that the rubber tree suffers under the continuing strain and the excessive loss of the precious bark brought about by the intensified harvest; and he may go on to point out that double panel tapping greatly aggravates the incidence of brown bast, a pernicious physiological affliction that leaves an otherwise healthy tree unable to replace the bark consumed by tapping. Far East rubber planters had never accepted double tapping as being permissible. It is true that some clones react to the severe milking more favorably than others; but, at least, double panel tapping reduces or severely strains the tree's ability to replace the lost bark, and bark is to a rubber tree what legs are to a chorus girl or fingers to a pianist. The Hevea tree's inability to replace the bark and the resulting disease of brown bast can force a great proportion of otherwise healthy trees out of bearing.

Fortunately for the United Nations, and particularly for Allied fighting forces to whom tires, tank treads, and other rubber wares spelled the difference between life and death, Firestone and citizen rubber growers of Liberia were the first and only important producing group who accepted the hazardous expedient of double panel tapping. This raised Liberia's output of rubber by millions of pounds. By the final war year Liberia's rubber production was almost double its total as of the date of Pearl Harbor; and, as already noted, every pound of it had gone directly to a U. S. Government procurement agency for allocation and distribution on a forthright basis of war-need priorities. Significantly, too, the natural rubber of Liberia, under severe price ceilings, had met optimum quality standards and, in terms of U. S. Treasury expenditures, had proved to be far and away the most economical rubber supply of which the United States was able to take advantage during the war years.

No less significant is the fact that Liberia's production of natural rubber is no longer limited to the Firestone plantations. It now includes groves planted and owned by approximately 140 citizen farmers of Liberia. Of that number about fifty native planters were together producing a yearly total of about 410,000 pounds of rubber (as of V-J Day), all of which was purchased by the Rubber Development Corporation for use in the United States. Also as of V-J Day, more than three-fourths of the rubber produced by citizen farmers of Liberia was being collected by double panel tapping.

Each year sees an increase in the total of natural rubber produced by civilian farmers. That Hevea rubber is now soundly established as a citizen crop of Liberia holds great promise for the future. Since 1939 all necessary planting material has been supplied to citizen growers from the nurseries of the Firestone Plantations Company. This venture began in 1939 with the distribution of 32,500 seedling "stumps" to interested farmers. For 1940 the tally climbed to 101,950. In 1941 it was 194,700 seedling stumps and 35,500 budded clonal trees. During 1942, as war needs for rubber loomed large and as Liberia formally joined the ranks of the United Nations, the distribution of budded Hevea trees to private farms climbed to 323,875. By 1947 the total of Hevea trees transferred from Firestone nurseries to privately owned farms and plantations had risen to 1,314,875 trees – enough to plant about 10,000 acres of bearing groves.

That total is not huge. But it plainly marks a milestone in the introduction of a new and complex crop. Already Liberia is producing about five times as much plantation rubber as is grown in all Central America, Mexico, the West Indies, and South America.

We still need natural rubber. As never before, and in ever-growing quantities, we need rubber, as do the other hundreds of millions of people whose very lives now depend on American production of goods. As this book is written, the total rubber supply which American manufacturers may rationally anticipate from trees, tubes, tanks, and factory lines together is somewhat more than one million tons a year. In past times we have found it easy to forget the desperate perils of rubber shortage — except when the shortage was perilously upon us. From now on, however, the cost of such forgetfulness may further multiply. Even disregarding future dangers, there is the certainty of greatly expanded future needs: America's needs for reliable and versatile rubber supplies, and Liberia's needs for more employment, greater earning power, and more abundant lives for her people.

Chapter Nine

Liberia and Africa

THE SUCCESSFUL and comparatively rapid introduction of the Hevea rubber tree as the decisive export crop of Liberia is an outstanding event of the present century. It is remarkable as a feat in crop introduction and still more remarkable as a feat in adaptation. When a highly technical, increasingly exacting world crop can be established without upsetting the frontier economy of a people, and without despoiling the indigenous social structure of the tribes, that is memorable news.

But the story of Liberia is also the story of a distinctive, vari-peopled frontier. For Liberia is also Africa — a crossroads on the world's second largest continent, an African melting pot. She is the home of twenty-three indigenous tribes and almost as many indigenous languages. Along the seafronts, roads, and trails of Liberia one can meet many other members of contemporary Africa: near neighbors and distant travelers, Liberia's own tribespeople and the population of American-Liberians.

From this crossroads it is possible to see a tremendous variety of African peoples. One may see the Chopis, an oval-faced, strongly Negroid people from the Portuguese colonies, music-loving, easy-going tribespeople who frequently stop by the roadside to eat fish and rice from their hands and drink water from wooden goblets. One occasionally sees the Kraals, decked out in their travelers' fineries — pantaloons and skirts made of softened oxhide, leather shirts, handbags brightly ornamented with braids and buttons.

And there are many clans of gaily robed Mandingos.

Now and then Sothos journey through — a particularly attractive people with a persisting fondness for grass-plaited hats fashioned like inverted buckets, and for white or blue cotton robes. As elsewhere in Equatorial Africa one sees the Fingos, an easy-going, pipe-puffing people, usually transient and homeless. They are likely to be wearing knitted skull caps and shoulder blankets, and as they walk their legs jingle with copper or bronze bands or anklets. The Anyanja people are one of the greatest farming peoples of all Africa, and the renowned African growers of American corn, rice, tobacco, and cotton.

Once in a great while one sees Thembus, a smallish, pug-nosed, thin-lipped people given to lining their faces with white and red ocher to suggest a happy expression, who wear symbolic necklaces and trade in cattle. Members of the Mzingili people appear, too — bushy-haired, thick-lipped, industrious, and artistic Africans who reputedly introduced Indian corn and maize and American types of sweet potatoes to Equatorial Africa, and who prove themselves outstanding workers in iron, copper, and bronze.

The Yao are also among the travelers from points south and east. For the most part they are Mohammedans, wearers of red fezzes frequently marked with copper or silver stars and feather plumes. The men usually wear loose, flowing robes in Mohammedan style. The women, too, wear toga-like robes, often exposing their midparts which are likely to be bizarrely tattooed. There are considerable numbers of Congo peoples, distinguished as builders and cabinet-makers, a few of whom have become Liberian citizens.

In Liberia, as in almost any other area of Equatorial Africa, one meets the heavy-featured, proud-postured Nyika — ambitious travelers, confirmed traders, and famed merchants of flake gold. For centuries the Nyika, whose original homeland was Portuguese East Africa, have been miners, metalsmiths, and far-roaming traders in metals. As Liberian finds of flake and other outcrop gold increase, so do the itinerant Nyikas.

The Ndaus are the great archers of Africa, master hunters with great bows and poison-tipped arrows. In the old days their hunting parties reportedly roamed westward as far as inland Liberia in pursuit of elephant herds and ivory. Robert Ripley might be interested to learn, if he has not learned already, that the Ndau have the ingenious custom of slashing complementary gashes on each of the shoulders and hips of young girls. The strips of skin are pried away from the flesh and shaped into permanent loops of skin. When a girl becomes a mother she has only to put her baby's hands and feet through the skin loops.

Like African scenery, soils, and climates, African peoples are infinitely varied. In many ways and in many voices the vast, often sad history of Africa is echoed in Liberia. Between the present site of Monrovia and the downcoast promontory of Cape Palmas were many of the principal slave trails and frontier slave depots which for almost two centuries supplied the most tragic cargo ever entered in international trade.

The vast majority of the enslaved Negroes brought to the United States were West Africans. Accordingly there is justice in the fact that the very land that saw so much of the white man's ruthless enslavement of his fellowman should have seen also the birth and growth of the one African nation that has undertaken the heroic experiment of democracy. Liberia as a republic actually antedates most of the major colonies and territories of West Africa. West Africa as a whole was "opened" late and darkly. Back in

1788, for example, the African Association was founded in London to sponsor trade between this remote part of the world and England and – in line with this objective – to solve the "mystery" of the Niger, then thought of as the fabulous river on whose banks stood the gold-spired city of Timbuktu. The African Association began sending explorers in the supposed general direction of the Niger. Of the first three "agents," two died of fevers and the third was murdered en route. In 1795-97 a fourth, a bold young Scot named Mungo Park, had better luck – at first. In December 1795 he started – dressed in a heavy blue coat and a tall beaver hat and accompanied by two Negroes – with only the vaguest idea of the direction he should take from Pisania, a British trading post on the Gambia River. His route crossed the upper Senegal basin and the semi-desert Kaarta region. At Ludamar he was imprisoned for four months by a Moorish chief, but in July 1796 he escaped, with nothing but his horse and a pocket compass, and presently reached the Niger at Segu – the first European to see the great river. After many difficulties he traced its course south and southeast for 300 miles, and then had to turn back, reaching Pisania again in June 1797.

Park then spent several years in England, always eager to return and explore the Niger basin all the way to its mouth on the Gulf of Guinea. In 1805 he made his second try, resolved to discover the mouth or "die on the Niger." And die he did. Encountering trouble with the natives early the next year after he had followed the stream for 1000 miles, Park and his three companions were drowned – precisely where and when is not known.

But the exploration of the bulge of Africa – that "White Man's Grave" – goes back to a considerably earlier date than Mungo Park's. Apparently the Portuguese were the first white men to invade it. The motive of the Portuguese explorations, which began early in the sixteenth century, was slave-trading: to capture and ship African people as slaves to the early tobacco and sugar plantations of the West Indies and other warmer fringes of the New World where white labor could not survive. Thus Portugal's entry into West Africa was strictly dishonorable, and so—in some sense—were the later entries of Spain, Holland, France, and Germany. In each case the magnet was the slaves, with the easy, tainted wealth they produced. The perpetuation of the slave trade, of course, involved the complete upset of all tribal affiliations among the slaves themselves and their descendants.

Such epigrammatic comments as "African roads start from London" or "Africa thinks with a British accent" are more than casual chatter. Indeed, they have significance for every African nation or people, Liberia included. The British hand first appeared in West African affairs around 1765, which was a banner year for empire grabbing. But even in 1765 a number of London "liberals" were strenuously urging the abandonment of the slave trade, and a number of titled servants of His Majesty's Government were already beginning to blush and stammer when the subject of the slave trade entered the conversation. Growing rich from slave-trading had ceased to be completely respected.

In 1772 Granville Sharp, a liberal barrister, began a seven-year lawsuit which terminated with Lord Chief Justice Mansfield's historic judgment that a liberated slave who sets foot on the land of England becomes a free man. The Mansfield verdict presently became a foundation document of British jurisprudence.

The story had begun when young Sharp took pity on a sick and whip-scarred West Indian Negro who had been abandoned on a London street. The studious barrister fed, clothed, and restored the penniless Negro to health, whereupon the slave was reclaimed by his master, a British subject, and sold back into slavery. The memorable lawsuit followed. Powerful West Indian planters, in collusion with wealthy and influential slave traders of London, Bristol, and Liverpool, bitterly challenged the Lord Chief Justice's decision. But the slavers lost their case and before the epochal judgment was finally confirmed England was being stirred by many anti-slavery leaders. Prominent among these was William Clarkson, who delighted in being called a muckraker and delivered ringing orations on the vile and deplorable conditions aboard the slave ships. He pointed out that most of Africa was being plagued and rotted by malicious slave traffic from the west, the east, and the north; from Cairo in Egypt and Goree Island off the West Coast to the Arab-kept slave pens along the Persian Gulf.

The eloquence of Clarkson and his sympathizers was effective. The British nation, to its untarnishable glory, led the world in embattled opposition to human slavery. In time the blood-spattered reports of slave revolutions in the French West Indies, particularly Haiti, gave momentum to British opposition at home. By 1807, Parliament formally passed an act declaring that beginning January 1, 1808, "all manner of dealing and trading in slaves" in Africa or in the transport of slaves from Africa to any other nation or area was to be "utterly abolished, prohibited and declared to be unlawful." Any British subject violating the act was to be heavily fined, and any British ship taking part in slave trade was forfeit. Even during the throes of its life-and-death struggle with Napoleonic France, the British Navy took over the formal enforcement of the prohibition of slave-running.

Shortly after the first Negro colonists had ventured upon

the coasts of Liberia, the British Parliament formally enacted the Abolition of Slavery Bill, and at the same time (August 29, 1833) appropriated the sum of twenty million pounds sterling to compensate all British-subject slave owners for their loss. This was one of the most enlightened enactments of the nineteenth century. But slavery, the greatest tragedy of Africa and Africans, lingered and, as already noted, the foundling nation of Liberia remained a tiny island in a vast black river of slavery.

France meanwhile had been moving into the north and west of Africa. The first French entry into West Africa began about 1767, when French slave traders, adequately assisted by the King's army and navy, began establishing or taking over slave-trade headquarters and claiming them for God, Louis, La Belle France, and the French slave-dealing plutocracy. In time the little island of Goree, off the Senegal coast, became France's number-one stronghold for slavers.

But from that same base a first group of French colonists moved to the mainland of Cape Verde (the present site of Dakar), and there persuaded the local Negro chiefs to sign X's to a treaty whereby on payment of a daily rental of 54 francs and one loaf of bread the adventurous French were entitled to found and occupy a first permanent colony in West Africa.

This first colonizing venture failed tragically. The Senegal countryside was infested with malaria and yellow fever, and successive slooploads of French colonists died. By 1817 all who had not perished of fevers had fled from Africa. But four years later, as the restored Bourbon regime began to gain strength, a handful of bold citizens from the southern farmlands of France ventured inland into Senegal and with the friendly permission of the chiefs and tribesmen began experimenting with developing gardens and grain farms. The particular hero of that venture was a market gardener's son named Jean Boudin who was first to introduce valuable European food crops to the Senegal area.

In time new bands of French farmers came and began to establish in Senegal what presently became the Dakar Colony. The adventure was essentially honorable as well as courageous and promised a new integrity in the white man's interest in Africa. Through trying years the farmers from France fought off the fevers and survived. They became acquainted and friendly with the Senegalese peoples, particularly the populous Walaf tribe, a docile and easy-going Mohammedan people, among whom the men still wear colorful flowing robes made of brilliant silks and strung with bright beads, as well as massive rings and bracelets, while the women display anklets that jingle with silver bells.

Thus from France's African stronghold of Dakar (or Cape Verde) French troops, traders, and colonists began fanning out through the vast interior lands of West and West Central Africa, making treaties with hundreds of tribal chiefs and native kings in many different realms. By 1866 the French government had completed a wharf and other harbor installations at Dakar and in 1878 began building a first railroad from Dakar to St. Louis, the inland capital of Senegal. (Readers may recall that at Goree Island during the darker days of World War II the British Navy took over the Vichy-fouled French fleet.)

By 1880 the Dakar area had become the real springboard for French entry and fortune-seeking in West Africa. The port city (with a native population of about 100,000) grew with additional thousands of French émigrés. The near-by farm lands yielded considerable quantities of food for the scattering waves of immigrants and the training garrisons for French troops, preponderantly native.

From Senegal more and more French troops, traders, and planters moved west and north into the vast Sudan where the grass grows tall and cattle flourish. Others followed farther west along the ancient trader trails and jungle paths into the upper Niger valley and the midlands of Chad, and on into the fringes of the lower Egyptian Sudan. Frenchmen wandered south and west to the Ivory Coast and still farther west and south to stake claim to the great head of French Equatorial Africa, including part of Cameroons, the Gabon coast, the Moyen boundary of the Congo, and the Dubangi country north of the huge Belgian Congo.

Few colonizing feats of man have been more daring or more consistently successful. The nineteenth century closed with a vast swirl of empire-grabbing. But France, with only about 60,000 troops, colonists, and traders all told, staked claims to and held more than two million square miles of Equatorial Africa; and in all Africa lands totaling about two-thirds the size of South America — lands in which at least 150 different languages were spoken. She maintained her hold through garrisons spaced in some instances more than a thousand miles apart, all the while earning profits for Paris, the empire, the traders, and some of the planters. By 1910 France's stake in West Africa was formidable in space and profits. By 1945 she had granted full citizenship to all African colonials. Today there are about eighty million citizens of France who are Africans.

Meanwhile Great Britain was also making African history. By 1815 Britain and Portugal had entered into an agreement whereby the latter agreed to limit her slave trade to points south of the equator. Two years later Spain agreed by formal treaty to the same terms. By 1818 France had declared the slave trade illegal for all French ships, and in 1820 Spain enacted a similar decree.

By 1820 the international slave trade had gone into the black-market, contraband stage. Slave-smuggling had grown wickedly profitable. Ports of the southern United States and the West Indies had been changed to capitals for this type of smuggling. On seas and shipping lanes, scalawag sailing ships loaded with the human cargo carried generous assortments of flags, so that whenever a British or a United States or a French naval vessel demanded the right to search, the slaver quickly hoisted an alien flag and went tranquilly on its way. The Republic of Liberia was born during the highest tide of slave trade and during a time of brazen defiance of "international laws" and marine police authorities.

Nevertheless, by gradual stages, Britain's man-of-war patrols of the West African coast became stronger and more persistent. Along the Liberian and neighboring coasts Kru tribesmen tattooed their foreheads or cheeks with a blue crescent or cross called the "Nelson mark" in an effort to inform the British patrols or anyone else that the wearer was a free African. In Liberia one still meets Krus tattooed with the now traditional Nelson mark.

As civil war grew closer in the United States, and as Liberian colonists struggled to stand against the jungle and isolation, one after another of the Latin American nations renounced the slave trade. Arab dhows began meeting more and more difficulties with the British Navy. Yet in Africa slave-raiding continued. Warlike tribes, bribed and supported by unscrupulous smugglers, continued to capture peaceful neighbors and tribesmen. Arab merchants kept up the cruel commerce, centering their activities on island plantations of the South Pacific and the huge spaces of the Middle East.

Abraham Lincoln's immortal Emancipation Proclamation was heard around the world, not excepting Africa. In 1876 at Zanzibar — then the slave capital of East Africa and the largest slave-trade center in the world — the native sultan formally prohibited all dealing in slaves within his domain and established the death penalty for violation. This proved to be the climax of the fight against slavery in Africa.

European interests in Africa at this time began shifting from slavery to colonies. Following the American Civil War a great rash of colonization societies and colonization companies began to appear in European capitals. In many instances these organizations were the obvious fronts for the well-studied aggrandizement plans of their respective governments. After the Franco-Prussian War, Germany swung strongly toward Africa, in some measure perhaps as a challenge to British supremacy in the Indian Ocean. By 1884 the German Colonization Society, for some years active in the Pacific tropics, advanced simultaneously into East Africa and West Africa.

The process of acquisition was traditionally one of so-called special treaties with the native chiefs. The chiefs, usually unacquainted with white men's languages, were prevailed upon by flattery, bribery, or threats, or a combination of them, to sign X's on documents purporting to transfer certain "civil amities" to the German society. After the chief had made his X, the German government would formally recognize the transaction as a valid concession and proclaim an imperial German protectorate over the area described, and frequently over adjoining territories for good measure. Again and again the so-called treaties were drawn with clan chiefs or other petty chiefs — without consulting the sultan or paramount chief of the area concerned. When the Sultan of Zanzibar protested that his subjects had no authority to sign away territory or concessions within his dominion, Bismarck dispatched a German battle fleet to subdue the Sultan. Unhappily, Britain (under Prime Minister Gladstone) did not interfere, perhaps because Bismarck had shrewdly played Britain against France.

During 1886, the Gladstone Government entered into treaty agreement with Bismarck's Government whereby Britain recognized a German sphere of influence in two strategic areas of the African East Coast, areas separated by an acknowledged British sphere of influence. But the inland boundaries remained vague. Karl Peters, Bismarck's Africa agent, set about squeezing the British-claimed protectorates from the East Coast and setting up the proposed German African kingdom of Uganda and the Upper Nile. However, by 1890 Germany, then seriously involved in French and Russian quarrels, hurriedly negotiated a treaty with Britain whereby in return for the island of Heligoland, Germany renounced all claims to East Africa outside of the Tanganyika area.

The game of power politics swept on, with Africa a principal playing field. By 1888 the British East Africa Company was industriously paving the British way throughout that part of the world. By 1893 Uganda, one of the many garden spots of Africa, had become a British protectorate, and by 1895 British protectorates extended along most of the rich East Coast.

Meanwhile, British involvements in the Sudan and upper Nile country had brought about a new structure of power politics. Through 1878 the Khedive Ismaïl had ruled Egypt under the nominal overlordship of the Sultan of Turkey. But Ismaïl's administration was unquestionably weak and grasping, and during 1882 France stepped in to take over the "chaotic finances of Egypt." Promptly, Britain intervened to establish "dual control." A revolt in the Egyptian army led the Gladstone Government to view with alarm a "lawless Egypt threatening the Suez Canal." British naval craft and Sir Garnet Wolseley's army overwhelmed the Arab rebels and captured Cairo. Thereafter the "dual control" became preponderantly British, and endured as such until 1922 when Egypt became an independent nation. (In 1936 the Anglo-Egyptian treaty of alliance reaffirmed British interest in the Suez Canal.)

However, for Africa as a whole, Britain's entry into Egypt marked the beginning of what British schoolbooks term "constructive imperialism." On the farther East Coast, in the lush Kenya protectorate, British engineers and financiers began building the Uganda Railway to link that strategic coast with the immensely resourceful interior. It was one of the most remarkable tales in the saga of railroading. Armies of imported laborers, principally from India, waded into a land of carnivorous crocodiles and man-eating lions. With relatively few exceptions the laborers survived these, but many thousands died of tropical fevers.

Meanwhile West Africa had known comparatively little colonial activity. Back in 1787, sixty years before Liberia declared itself a sovereign republic, the British Government had established Sierra Leone immediately upcoast from Liberia, as a refuge colony for freed slaves of the Empire. With time and persuasion, West Indian and other Negroes settled on some of its coastal lands much as Negroes from the United States were later to come to the seafront of Liberia.

But speaking generally, the white man's hold in West Africa remained feeble until late in the nineteenth century. Because of tropical fevers, the solemn title "White Man's

Grave" became more and more widely used to designate the immense West Coast. But West Africa was far too rich in potential resources to be avoided indefinitely. In along the West Coast, the Germans began grabbing off the fertile and attractive lands adjoining the Cameroon mountains. Also, north and west, inland from the Gold Coast, the fierce tribal wars of the Ashantis broke out anew.

During 1872 the Ashanti army, reputedly 40,000 strong, crossed the Prah River, overwhelmed the Fantis (a tribe then in British protectorate), and took over the British-held port of Elmina. At that point, and not by accident, a British warship and other battlecraft arrived. Promptly Captain John Glover and Sir Garnet Wolseley landed a force of Royal Marines and organized an army of defending tribesmen whose spears and bows they supplemented with British firearms and ammunition. Under English leadership the jungle-edge army proceeded against the Ashantis, defeated their army, and in 1874 enforced a treaty of surrender. Later the Ashantis returned to fight again – whereupon British forces abolished the Ashanti "monarchy" and joined it with the Gold Coast Colony.

The driving force of all this was the desire for trade. Frontier merchants, independents as well as companies, had learned and proved that African trade was enormously profitable to the trader – as it still is. High profits on the goods in stock could be doubled or tripled by profits collectible on crops and merchandise gained from the natives by processes of barter. More and more French, German, and British traders were filtering into the West African frontiers. In 1879 the British traders began grouping themselves into an association that eventually developed into the huge imperial corporation, the United Africa Company. During 1886 another charter corporation, the Royal Niger Company, was born with Downing Street encouragement, and commissioned as Her Majesty's administrator of the rich and populous lands of the Niger valley. Fourteen years later the Royal Niger Company was shorn of its administrative powers and privileges, and refurbished (to nobody's surprise) as the British Protectorate of Northern and Southern Nigeria.

With that the international scramble for West Africa became still more frenzied. France attached "treaty claims" to the upper Niger, and to all the huge spaces now called French West Africa and French Equatorial Africa. The two strongest contenders were well checkmated. British acquisitions included the resourceful but little-developed coastal strips along the Gambia River, of Sierra Leone, the Gold Coast, Lagos, and Nigeria. Yet plainly, by 1900, still another purpose began to appear in British policy. The era of slave-catching had been replaced by an era of colony-grabbing, which in turn was being replaced by an era of studied development through trade – trade enormously profitable to the British, but nevertheless welcomed by a majority of native Africans.

Captain Frederick J. D. Lugard and others of Her Majesty's men set about strengthening the British West African position by what they termed the "system of indirect rule," a strategy aimed at least in some part toward leading Africans to lead themselves. As the first British governor of comparatively densely populated Nigeria, Lord Lugard, who was a sickly little man with exceptional talents for listening, laid down his own interpretation of British policy: "Britain accepts as its moral obligation to administer colonial territories in such a way that the latter's resources are developed on the one hand for the benefit of the native inhabitants, and on the other for the benefit of the world at large." Lord Lugard held steadfastly to this tenet until his death in 1940.

But not all Britishers who went into what the home newspapers continued to term the "White Man's Grave" represented Her Majesty's fighting forces or Her Majesty's Colonial Office. There were, as there still are, many splendid missionaries, teachers, physicians, and other immensely worthwhile civilians. Dr. David Livingstone, and his renowned missionary career in another area of the continent, inspired others to do likewise in West Africa. For example, there was Mary Slessor who came to the West Coast in 1876 and stayed for thirty years, ministering to the sick, acting as judge and counsel in native courts, and teaching and helping the tribespeople. She worked in Nigeria near the banks of the River Cross, far from white man's comforts, luxuries, and laws. In far-scattered jungle communities other pioneer missionaries from the British Isles, the United States, Germany, and Scandinavia followed in the gallant Slessor tradition. Some failed in their charges, but many more succeeded.

On the whole, Britain's establishment of colonies in West Africa merged conspicuous faults with conspicuous merits. Millions of Africans were obliged to accept the bad with the good. In any case several trends were outstanding. British colonial administration sought to build up trade. British influence in West Africa as a whole was preëminent. And from the Africans' standpoint British colonial activities were best in the broad fields of humanities and nonofficial relations – not in politics or military operations.

British achievements were headlined by distinguished findings in preventive medicine. Sir Ronald Ross of the British Army Medical Service in India, who had been first to discover that the anopheles mosquito is the carrier of malaria (then as now the foremost cause of sickness and death in Africa as in most other tropics), led the splendid parade of British-directed research in West Africa. Ross's epochal findings were first announced in 1895, and brilliantly confirmed by his later researches in the Gambia Basin and the malaria-infested frontiers of Sierra Leone in West Africa. Malcolm Watson, his brilliant disciple, carried on the great work, and in the Gambia Basin and other West African lowlands pioneered the use of oil sprays and field-sanitation devices to protect people from disease-bearing mosquitoes.

During the 1890s, two other British medical pioneers, David Bruce and Charles Swynnerton, came to West Africa to open their struggle against the tsetse fly and sleeping sickness. Bruce, who like Ronald Ross was a member of the British Army Medical Service, came to West Africa in 1894. There he watched horses and cattle die of the mysterious parasitic disease within a few days or hours. He observed, too, that uncounted thousands of West African people were dying of what seemed to be the same disease. Bruce traced the cause of the "malady of excessive slumber" to a parasite carried in the digestive tract of a common African fly with wings conspicuously barred with yellow and veined with red.

Bruce then traveled into Uganda, where the ominous malady had brought death to at least 20,000 tribesmen within one year. He was unable to complete the great work. Swynnerton carried on. Born in England in 1877, Swynnerton came to Nigeria as a boy to work as a helper in a jungle-front commissary. But he became interested in the insects, birds, and plant life of the world about him, thus changing over from merchandising to science. He took a three-month holiday to study the bewildering tsetse fly. From that time he "took over," usually alone, substantially self-trained and self-made, coördinating his talents as an amateur naturalist with his devoted study of medicine and the new science of pathology. In time he was able to prove beyond any reasonable doubt that the pretty bush fly with the yellow-barred, red-veined wings is indeed the carrier of sleeping sickness, which can be controlled when and if the fly is destroyed.

The phenomenon which the London newspapers had begun calling the "New Era of Africa" demonstrated still other constructive talents of the British. Even in 1900, one traveled in West Africa at the imminent peril of his life—either toiling up the rivers by dugout canoe or light launch, or tramping the rough and narrow bush trails, or riding in a wagging hammock borne on the heads of native carriers. Drums were the only effective means of communication. Tribes that for generations had lived only fifty miles apart had never actually seen each other. Sudden floods, storms, or invasion by elephant herds frequently left the members of one tribe to starve, while tribesmen a few miles away had wasted surpluses of rice and other foods.

During the decade between 1900 and 1910, British engineers and British investment capital, abetted by native and imported labor, completed approximately 15,000 miles of railroad in Equatorial Africa, including some of the most difficult construction in railroading history. First lines of steel pushed across fierce rivers, through man-ruining jungles and virulent malaria swamps, into the playgrounds and feeding lands of wild elephants, leopards, and gorillas. During that one decade railroad lines appeared in every one of Britain's West African colonies except Gambia. During the same ten years, railroad construction in France's Ivory Coast Colony and the Dakar area and other parts of French West Africa had totaled about 4,000 miles. Significantly, the average cost of railroad construction in West Africa was approximately twice that of the same type of construction in East Africa.

Along with or immediately after the first railroads into the West African wilds, British and French government men and contractors began building highways and military roads which as a rule are even more difficult and costly to build than railroads. In general, Africa remains gravely lacking in highways, and the road systems of West Africa are particularly inadequate. Nevertheless thousands and more thousands of miles of foot trails are being transformed to motor roads, mainly through tribal labor, sponsorship by local chiefs, and revenues raised locally by the colonies. West African communications, too, have benefited immensely by recent impressive developments in air transportation. At present, between Dakar and Cameroons, West Africa has in use forty year-'round air fields or flying-boat bases.

British colonial enterprises also included harbor-building for a great coastline that is lacking in natural harbors. Unfortunately for West Africa these harbor works were too long delayed. One of the first, at Takoradi on Britain's Gold Coast, was opened in 1928 to provide Gold Coast manganese with a way to the sea. That port gave a preview of West African mineral wealth and proved immensely valuable in supplying Allied forces during the African campaigns of World War II.

British talent has also helped memorably in developing West African farming. The venture began with the commercial opening of the lower Niger valley, which is one of the world's great reservoirs of palm oil. Early British traders promptly seized on the indigenous African oil-palm crop as a staple for barter and frontier merchandising. Millions of tribal people relied on the nutritious oil as a food staple, as they still do. The compact and comparatively non-perishable nut is portable even in roadless countries — as head burdens or as cargo for native boats. And palm oil is a tropical commodity that industrial nations require for the manufacture of lather soap, shampoos, and fine margarines, for metallic plating, industrial glycerine, and many other staple needs.

Also under British auspices cacao became the first "introduced crop" of West Africa. Back in 1886 workers of the British Colonial Office dispatched cacao (cocoa) seed from Venezuela and Central America to government nurseries of the Gold Coast where the seeds were planted under Colonial Office supervision. When the silver-dappled seedlings were ready for transplanting, colonial agronomists began distributing the young trees to chiefs throughout the Gold Coast area. A number of paramount chiefs adopted the new alien crop and set out to teach their tribesmen how to grow and process it. In 1891, after five experimental years, the port of Accra made a first export of eighty pounds of cacao. Within forty years the first eighty pounds had climbed to approximately a quarter-million tons of the raw chocolate "beans," which are being grown on approximately a third of a million orchards ranging in size from several hundred acres down to a few square yards and scattered throughout thousands of miles of the great Rain Forest. Gold Coast cacao farms supply at least half of all chocolate consumed in the United States.

Cotton has become another instance of a "developed" crop for West Africa. As recently as 1903 all the cotton harvested along the West Coast was from low-yielding wild varieties. During that year the Colonial Government of Nigeria purchased a first half-ton of selected long-staple cotton seed in the United States, distributed these seeds among the chiefs, and established a tremendously promising industry of cotton.

With passing years more and more steps in agricultural progress have been made directly by the Africans. Sisal, coffee, ginger, beeswax, and sugar cane are among new crops that West African farmers and chiefs have developed through their own efforts and resources.

With time and trial-and-error, Britain's Colonial Government in West Africa has grown into a pattern. Each one of His Majesty's African colonies has a central government headed by a Crown-appointed governor-general, responsible to the Secretary of State for the Colonies in London. The Governor-General presides over a law-making and tax-raising legislative council and an executive council. All council members are Africans. There are also regional or provisional councils in which chiefs and other tribe members serve.

Even during 1940, when the Empire stood at death's door, Parliament appropriated about a quarter-billion dollars for research and development for the colonies and supplemented the proposed ten-year plan with a special "act for Africa" which launched, as of April 1946, an African "self-benefit programme." The latter undertaking assists in farm experimentation, enterprises in disease control, the building of new schools and public hospitals, and – most important – the training of native Africans to staff and perpetuate these facilities. At the present time, in upper Nigeria, one of the greatest organized campaigns against sleeping sickness is now in progress under combined British and African leadership.

This work, like the "self-benefit programme" as a whole, is admirable. But one can list altogether too many examples of tragic and deplorable lack of official understanding and adaptability in British West African possessions. In general the postwar colonial administration of French Africa has lagged and faltered badly, not so much because of the intentions of colonial administrators as from the disintegration of France. And all Africa has suffered a profound upset from another great European war. Postwar worries and tensions continue to create confusion and paradoxes in colonial policies. Today Portuguese, Spanish, and German colonial policies in Africa are almost uniformly disgraced and discredited. The Belgian Congo, strongly industrialized and comparatively tranquil, retains an enviable solvency. But, speaking generally, after a world-shattering war in which the "mother nations" fought, sweated, and bled for survival, the trials and agonies of all empires were inevitably passed on to the colonies, and Africa is a continent of colonies.

All this tends to center the spotlight even more strongly on Liberia. It memorializes the fact that throughout a stormy century Liberia with incredible endurance has pioneered a way for sovereign independence in a continent wherein independence has remained almost nonexistent.

Chapter Ten

Liberia and Medicine

THOUGH CHRONICALLY and desperately short of physicians and surgeons, Liberia is a stronghold of folk medicine, which is a part of the tribe commune and is endlessly challenging to medical scholars the world over. Born of a violent natural environment, it is a mixture of long-lived traditions, local philosophies, and religious credos; of fear, hope, and everyday expedients. To the imaginative man or woman of medicine Liberia is a clinic and a laboratory of pharmacology, surgery, specific therapies, and long-tested psychiatric practices.

Liberia has great usefulness for the medical world of today and tomorrow, and in turn she urgently requires the knowledge, facilities, and services of modern medicine. Perhaps no living physician is better qualified to speak of these problems than George Way Harley, M. D., medical missionary and founder-director of the impressive jungle-edge clinic in the tribal countryside of Ganta.

During a rich lifetime of work in backcountry Liberia, Dr. Harley has served and taught the tribespeople. He has tended tens of thousands of the sick and distressed and mingled surgery, obstetrics, clinical medicine, and emergency practice. Like all good physicians, he has learned a great deal from his patients. I am particularly indebted to Dr. Harley for much of the material of the following pages.

Folk medicine of Liberia is born of folk philosophy. As the backcountry tribesmen see it, every living person has several souls. One is his shadow; another is his dream soul (which the Manos call *zu*) ; another is the soul that is man's breath; and there is also the body soul which after death lingers near by for a time, but presently leaves the body and goes to God's town which is far away.

Apparently the several souls of man are not very clearly distinguishable. Singly or collectively they may be worshipped as ancestral spirits, and they may at times be recalled by sacrifice or prayer. In any case the soul is shepherd to the living flesh.

Good health is the natural state and the heritage of man. Disease is unnatural, an intrusion of outside forces directed by magical or superhuman forces which must be rationalized and understood by the individual. Accordingly, the Liberian tribe member is ever a philosopher. To him the very mountaintops are sacred as living things; so are the sun, the moon, the nearer planets, and the Milky Way. He is clearly convinced that every object, whether animate or inanimate, has a spirit within it. Therefore a good and knowing man may talk to a tree or a rock or to a river or cliff or mountain with the conviction that the spirit hears, the spirit that is part of the object. It is entirely appropriate for a tribesman to seek fleetness from the spirit of a wind-blown leaf, or to plead for strength from the spirit of a hard rock. Any substance whose power is thus controlled by its spirit is "medicine." In the Mano tribe's language the word is *Nye,* and any means for channeling or directing the power is *Nye ke,* which means "making medicine." The person who makes the medicine is *Nye ke mi,* the doctor.

Dr. Harley explains more adequately: "*Nye* is that which has more power than a casual examination might reveal. *Nye* is any substance or fetish used in making medicine or controlling illness. . . . Certain rare and precious medicines are thought to have sight and speech, even the ability to assume human form and move about. . . . The latter is a fetish, a living thing in its own right, an object for prayer or sacrifice, or both. . . ."

A typical fetish is a *zang,* an oval cone-shaped object hand-molded of fiber and clay and sometimes smeared with eggs and fragments of eggshells. The *zang* requires a particular fare each month (such as a hen egg served just as the new moon appears). The owner is usually obliged to supplement this sustenance by making a specific sacrifice to the fetish, such as killing a chicken in its particular honor.

The fetish, if and as it chooses to do so, can travel about in human form saying pleasant things about its owner and helping him to prosper and keep healthy. But, manlike, the *zang* may become tired and sluggish. In that case the owner is inclined to stimulate it by means of such routines as taking a grain of hot pepper, chewing it with a mouthful of cola nut, then spitting the mixture over the fetish.

Prayers and sacrifices are both routine and spontaneous: prayers to mother earth at the time of planting crops so that she will not stint the harvest of rice, cotton, palm nuts, and other good crops; prayers to the waterfalls, which are the homes of the rainbow serpents that make lands fertile; to the trees inhabited by human souls; to the sacred hills where the great rains live; or to fire and iron. The masks, particularly the *Ma,* mother of all masks, are usually symbolic of religion which is a phase of medicine.

The "witch doctor" is a priest, a physician, and a would-be or real philosopher whatever his tribe. The Kpelle reveres his wayside shrine. The Mano marks his sacred trees, one of which is bombax or mahogany, and at the grave of his father he plants the cola palm, a venerated spirit tree.

The doctor-priest always proceeds on the principle that life is lasting and that death is some manner of accident which the living are in duty bound to try to overcome.

Zo, another Liberian tribal word for doctor, combines priesthood, midwifery, medicine, divinity, and philosophy. Significantly *Zos* may also be women. As a rule the *Zo* or witch doctor avoids explaining his medicine to the patient, because he believes (or at least suspects) that the sickness may be a spirit that is capable or hearing and thus of counteracting the medicine proposed.

The duty of the native doctor is to attend the sick and to seek to make them well, and he has surprising means at his disposal. Frequently he gives enemas with long-necked gourds, uses reeds for urethra, applies poultices, administers medicated baths, improvises splints, and sets fractures — all with outstanding skill. Dr. Harley recalls this instance:

> "At Ganta in 1927, a Bassa boy was thrown violently by a Kisi wrestler, landing on one foot and suffering a Pott's fracture. The white doctor applied a plaster-of-paris splint in the approved fashion. The reputation of the local Mano specialist in fractures was greater than that of the white doctor. The boy had the plaster removed. The native specialist applied a light coadaptation splint made of split raffia midrib. He removed the latter daily and massaged the foot with an astringent paste which dried on like a coat of stiff glue. The splints were reapplied each day. After a week the patient was urged to use the foot lightly. The aim was for a useful member rather than a perfect alignment. The final result was as good as could be expected. There was no deformity. The boy walked without limping, but said he got tired on a long journey. . . .*

**Native African Medicine,* by G. W. Harley, Harvard University Press, 1944, Cambridge, Mass.

The native pharmacology is important and often useful. Usually the tribal medical man devises potions of native herbs for treating such nuisance diseases as bacillary dysentery and common flesh ulcers. Frequently he treats severe wounds by poulticing them with selections of native leaves which probably have curative values. Many *Zos* make tourniquets to stanch severed arteries, drain abscesses, and show outstanding skill in the use of counterirritants.

Extremely few witch doctors attempt internal surgery, though tragically this is desperately needed for hernia, filariasis, and many other troubles of the tribespeople. But other basic medical needs have been recognized. For example, the working principles of quarantine have long been known to the native doctors, at least some of whom have recognized – presumably for centuries – that many common diseases are contagious. When a tribe member is stricken with smallpox, for example, he is moved to a "sick bush" or pest house, usually an improvised shack some distance from the village or the nearest home.

There the sick man stays in comparative isolation. If the illness is severe, one attendant, usually a wife or other family member, may share his isolation. Other relatives or friends bring food and drink which they leave at a convenient distance. The invalid is severely confined to quarters. If he breaks away prematurely or otherwise violates the taboo, he cannot expect to recover from the disease. With tragic frequency isolation cases die of neglect. But such are the vagaries of African arts of healing.

For many African peoples the measurement of time is difficult or impossible. Sometimes when a smallpox sufferer is quarantined, a young rooster, preferably a red one, is placed near the patient, who is told that when the rooster is big enough to crow he may leave the sick bush.

Various theories and practices for feeding the sick are also noteworthy. Frequently the sick man's diet consists of sugar cane, a sweet palm oil for restoring strength, and one of several brews of soups as tonics. Where money is scarce, or nonexistent, doctor's fees are usually paid in barter, plus a "dash" for good measure; sometimes, as a final bounty—as in smallpox cases—the medicine man is permitted to take the rooster home and eat it.

Like their colleagues throughout most of the world, the tribal medicine men of West Africa were flabbergasted by the pandemic of influenza that swept over Africa and most of the rest of the world during 1918-19. Dr. Harley tells of an especially studious Mano medicine man who dreamed of the "right" medicine to combat the virulent flu germ. The potion consisted of a handful of genezola thorns *(Combretum aculeatum)* burned to charcoal, then ground to powder, mixed with red palm oil, and rubbed on the ankles, knees, and elbows of the sufferer. One gathers that the dream remedy proved about as effective as any other influenza remedy of that period.

Indigenous Liberian medicine treats fevers with teas brewed of lemon grass, lime juice, or "feverleaf," which the Manos call *geazu* and the botanists call *Ocimum confusa.* The inner bark of a small tree called *mo a yidi* may be used, or the leaves of a bushy vine called *yini za (Morinda confusa)* to which is added a small quantity of "country salt," actually a crystalline potash lye made by leaching wood ashes.

Measles, which is common throughout most of Africa, is usually treated with the leaves of the cotton tree beaten to a pulp and mixed with white clay or kaolin which in turn is diluted with water to form a paste. The measles sufferer smears the paste over his body and sleeps alone in the open.

Each morning he bathes himself with water strained from the leaf pulp, then reapplies the clay paste. As the rash begins to disappear, the patient returns to the standby African treatment of a daily hot bath, after which palm oil, flavored with various aromatic herbs, may be rubbed into the skin.

Quite appropriately, whatever the ailment may be, if the patient wilfully violates the medicine man's instruction, the latter cannot be held responsible for the patient's failure to recover. If the patient dies, the bush doctor is obliged to replenish and appease his fetish; if his professional score continues excessively bad, the medicine man is eventually forced out of his trade either by order of the chief or the elders or by a determined boycott by the tribal clientele.

Rheumatism, prevalent in most tropical countries, is usually treated with liniments, such as those made by mixing together soft clays and water, particularly the gray clays recovered from ant hills—possibly with a content of formic acid—and lime leaves or other kinds of leaves that are beaten to pulp. After the liniment is removed, the patient, lying prostrate on a bed of heated leaves, is treated with an application of a soothing powder. Counterirritation is also a common strategy for treating rheumatism.

Headaches are treated by binding the forehead tightly with a slender vine. The tribespeople eat cola nuts which contain caffein to gain a mild stimulant and stomachic and to overcome extreme fatigue. A common diuretic is made from the dried bark of the *bo* tree *(Mitragyna stipulosa)*, which is ground or beaten to a powder, carefully sifted, and diluted with hot water or palm wine.

The respiratory diseases are among the gravest enemies to Africa today; particularly the common cold, bronchitis, pneumonia, and tuberculosis. This last vies with malaria as

Liberia's number-one enemy of health, and plainly it is entirely beyond the reach of native medicine. As elsewhere the common cold is the most frequent disease. As a cold cure the jungle medicine man or woman takes the root of a common perennial called *suo longo (Ethulia conyzoides),* cuts the root into small pieces, adds hot capsicum peppers and potash salt, boils the mixture well, and lets it cool over night. Each morning the cold sufferer drinks one or two cupfuls of the brew.

The boiled root of the *goa* bush is a common remedy for biliousness and colic. For intestinal worms, another frequent cause of debility throughout West Africa, small green figs prove an effective vermifuge where and if that native fruit is available. Otherwise the medicine man may take strips of the inner bark of corkwood (*wolo* to the Mano and *Musanga Smithii* to botanists), add the seed of *dua di (Aframonium Baumanii),* then beat the mixture to a fine pulp and dilute it with cold water. A purgative dose of half a teacupful is usually effective for ridding a child of intestinal worms. For adults the ascarids are usually expelled by having the sufferer eat especially prepared dishes, such as the buds of the *woma* tree *(Trema guniesis)* mixed with a meat dish or cooked plantains, washed down with a vermifuge made by boiling finely beaten *ti mana (Millettia sanagana)* root in water.

A considerable number of these remedies are pharmaceutically sound and therefore of enduring value. Many distinguished medical observers approve such jungle standbys as that of treating deep bruises with a strong tea made from a native grass called *duo su (Eleusine india);* or easing a sore throat with portulaca leaf *(Portulaca oleracea)* beaten up with dried ginger root and served in an appetizing broth or soup.

Frequently the jungle medicine men use slippery-elm bark as a substitute for quinine for treating malaria. (During World War II, Liberian supplies of therapeutic quinines were promptly and completely exhausted.) Another native Liberian remedy that is now being investigated by medicinal-plant experts is the oil of the "woodnut" which many backcountry Liberians eat. About a quarter-century ago this nut was exported extensively for use in making varnish oil. In the treatment of leprosy it seems closely similar to and perhaps more valid than chaulmoogra oil, the long-used leprosy remedy whose curative value is now being challenged. Several native rotenone-bearing roots or "fish poison medicines" are respected and used widely as insecticides for crops and as vermin removers for both human beings and livestock.

The pharmacy of the Liberian interior arises from the life-crowded jungle. Some of its lore and findings have already proved beneficial to international medicine and pharmacy, and it is a safe prediction that their overall value is certain to increase.

Many of the native concepts of disease belong in the realm of magic. Dr. H. C. Trowell, writing for the *East African Medical Journal,* comments: "The African child is reared in a world where ghosts are more real than men, a world controlled by spirits. . . . Magical conception and magical causations become the facts of his philosophy. The pleasure or anger of the spirits is the cause of all disease, famine, death, and the whole range of natural science." *

But even the magical treatment of disease, as one sees it in the interior of Liberia, involves a considerable amount of

*" Medical Training of Africans," H. C. Trowell, *East African Medical Journal,* 1935, No. 2, p. 338.

folk logic in diagnostics and frequently opens the way for notable uses for psychotherapy. For example, hunchback is taken to be the result of evil magic and accordingly its treatment is magical. There is a common jungle tree called *kue (Pentaclethra macrophylla Bent)* which invariably grows with a hump or a twist in its trunk. The tribal medicine man converses with the spirit of the tree, after which he takes a rock and beats off some of the tree's bark. Then he pounds the bark into clay, seasons it with pepper seed, and rubs the paste over the hump of the hunchback.

This, like the craw-craw treatment, is obviously "magic." The ulcers of craw-craw are supposed to afflict one who has eaten leopard's flesh in violation of a taboo. Therefore to cure the disease the sufferer cooks some rice, places it on a leaf, then calls a cat to eat the rice. For a cat, according to tribal ideas, is nothing more or less than a miniature leopard. After the cat has eaten, the sufferer finishes whatever rice is left over, saying as he eats it, "Craw-craw, go finish one time!" (*One time* means right away.)

Leprosy is sometimes treated with the inner bark of the *bi* tree, mixed with water. The solution is rubbed on the skin and dropped into the ulcers. This, presumably, is "magic."

Like most of West Africa, rural Liberia is afflicted with a number of poisonous snakes, though they are not nearly so numerous as popular fiction represents. One of the most feared is the green mamba, which particularly during mating season hides in the tops of palm trees and takes lethal vengeance on any unfortunate man or woman who comes to gather the palm nuts. The accepted first-aid practice is to pull out a handful of the tender leafbuds of the oil palm, chew up the heart end, and, with this in the mouth, suck out the poison; then, as soon as the wound ceases to bleed, to open it with a knife.

Other variously poisonous snakes are the black cobra; the *bina,* a small black snake that frequently invades family huts in search of mice; the *gbala* or night adder; and a long red snake called *gba lono.* A common preliminary to treating snakebite is to require the victim to vomit by administering an herb emetic, then to pick several leaves from a *wana* tree *(Mareya spicata),* chew them and, holding the leaf pulp in the mouth, suck the wound, then spit out the poison. Then the snake doctor takes more of the same kind of leaves, bruises them, places the mass on the wound, and uses a strip of *wana* bark to make a tourniquet which he ties snugly over the bite.

In some backcountry areas of Liberia the treatment of snakebites has become a specialized vocation supported by a secret society which in some of the interior villages maintains cult houses and ritual grounds far out in the forests. The candidate must purchase membership, master the cult ritual, and by progressive stages learn how to tame snakes, however poisonous or ill-tempered, and how to make them lethargic. To accomplish this he may chew up leaves of the *sei* tree *(Microdesmis puberula)* and spit the saliva mixture on the snake's head. This makes the reptile groggy and listless, and no doubt helps the would-be snake doctor to overcome his own fear of the snake.

Punitive medicine is still another phase of jungle psychotherapy. Dr. Harley has reported a technique for correcting and punishing a woman who has a "big mouth"—who is loud and insolent. The medicine man begins by taking a young shoot of *fai (Manniophyton africanum)* and picking off the leaves, speaking a magic word for each leaf removed.

Then, using his left hand he strips the leaves from a branch of *pu (Deinbollia piniate)* in the same way. He beats up the double handful of leaves and rolls the mass over the ground where the woman has urinated. Then he makes up a packet of plantain leaves and drops this on the woman from the loft of her hut, the object being to bring about a bladder irritation. In time the woman pleads with the man of magic to make her well. He agrees, terminates his magic, and the next day the woman is cured both of her polyuria and of her loudness and insolence. At least, that is what the Mano witch doctor says.*

Native medicine, like so much of the enduring life of Liberia, is bound up with ritual. Medicine enters into certain phases of the ritualistic schools for tribal youth, the Sande school for young girls, and the Poro school for adolescent boys, which are conducted and taught by respected elders or priestesses or priests of the tribe. The ritualistic tribe schools, though not well known to outsiders, do actually give the youngsters instruction in elementary first-aid practices, black magic, jungle pharmacology, and traditional cures. And back of the frontier clinics and Poro schools there are at least the remnants of several persistent black-magic societies such as the Leopard Society, whose members – slightly disguised by capes of leopard skins, their hands concealing iron claws resembling leopard teeth–spring out to murder unwary victims whose remains are used sacrificially by the order. Generally similar though less widespread are the Crocodile Society and the Python Society. These evil cults have been unduly publicized because they are sensational.

During recent years, fortunately, such menaces have been

**Native African Medicine,* G. W. Harley.

greatly diminished by the persistent, valiant police work of the Liberian government and the public courts, which have repeatedly dealt prompt and stern punishment to convicted members of the killer cults. The Leopard Society is not entirely stamped out, however, and many Liberian people still walk in fear of Leopard Men and real leopards as well. But the cause for fear is gradually abating.

It is true, too, that jungle medicine and magic have been put to other illicit uses. There was, for example, the Mano Cult of Thieves whose members reputedly used potent medicines to protect themselves from arrest or capture while stealing. But the medicines were not strong enough to impress the government's courts.

The use of noxious herbs to establish guilt or to prove innocence is still in ritualistic use in many rural areas. The most common example is trial by sasswood, which—at least to the newcomer—is a bewildering institution. In various tribal courts anyone accused of a crime is still permitted to elect "trial by sasswood." By tradition, the accused mounts a platform or sits before those assembled to pass judgment. He then undergoes the sasswood ordeal, which consists in drinking varying amounts, usually at least six cupfuls, of a heavy tea brewed from the bark of the sasswood or *gli* tree *(Erythrophleum guineense)*. According to folk belief, if the accused is innocent he will vomit up the fluid, which has considerable emetic quality. If guilty he is unable to vomit, becomes ill, and frequently dies of the dosage, which presently acts as a violent cathartic.

The various ritualistic formalities connected with sasswood trial may serve to heighten its psychological efficacy. In any case, it frequently happens that tribesmen who are accused of crimes and maintain their innocence voluntarily request trial by sasswood. This institution of justice is decidedly challenging to the psychiatrist, the physician, the jurist, or the student of legal history.

Cults, Poro schools, secret societies, sasswood ordeals—these are essentially parts of jungle lore, not science. Nevertheless Liberia has a great deal to offer the arts of medicine and hygiene. One is impressed by the cleanliness of the native peoples, their never-ending hot baths and cold baths, daily or twice daily; the habitual cleanliness of their huts; their conscientious removal of "night soil" and filth; their diligence in cleansing their teeth (using raffia fibers in lieu of toothbrushes); their wistfully gallant struggles against the great disease enemies that would destroy them. Native therapies, pharmacology, and practical hygiene have helped the Liberian tribes to survive in a country where physicians and surgeons with formal degrees and professional experience are tragically scarce, and where in some areas regularly qualified doctors of medicine are hundreds of miles apart.

By extremely gradual stages the number of formally educated physicians increases. But the two million people of Liberia today are desperately in need of medical facilities and services. They remain dependent on native lores and cures which, however ingenious, are sadly inadequate.

Typical of the overall plight is the condition of the great Mah or Mano nation, which includes a substantial part of north central Liberia and parts of French West Africa in the valleys of the St. John and the Ya rivers. There are probably about 200,000 Manos. At the present time the entire fifth of a million have access to only two medical practitioners who have accredited medical training and professional degrees.

South and east of the Ya, in the same green hilly country, are the Geh and Gio tribes, and beyond them the great

Kpelle nation, all of whom are still dependent chiefly on native medical facilities for obstetrics, pediatrics, elementary sanitation, pan-and-mortar pharmacy, general surgery, and epidemiology. In such places and circumstances the value of folk medicine is inevitably great. But in the world today, where epidemics travel with the speed of planes and plane passengers, where so many deadly diseases take their final refuge in the deep tropics, and where the migration of people so frequently occasions a similar migration of lethal disease, there is overwhelming need for medical services, facilities, and research. Like most of Equatorial Africa, Liberia remains under constant and appalling threat of illness.

A small minority of the prevalent diseases, such as sleeping sickness and certain types of dysentery or hookworm, are confined largely to the tropics. But the problem does not lie in such comparatively localized diseases; rather it lies in defending native peoples against cosmopolitan, world-spanning disease. The findings acquired in the great tropical laboratory of Liberia can benefit people of all countries. Distinguished research groups such as the Louis Pasteur Institute, the Rockefeller Institute, and the London School of Tropical Medicine have already taken advantage of these possibilities. More recently the American Foundation for Tropical Medicine has undertaken the sponsorship of a research institute in Liberia—an undertaking of still greater promise.

One realizes the opportunities as well as the size of the job still to be done when he examines the magnificent work contributed by George Way Harley and his little mission at Ganta. One senses it, too, when meeting such men as the bush doctor far out on the French Guinea frontier who calls himself Cavally Jones. "Boss" Jones has given a third of a century of his life to attending the sick and the dying without fee or recompense beyond the satisfaction of having served suffering humanity. Though lacking a degree from an accredited medical college, he is at least able to recognize serious sickness or the need for surgery, and to deliver sick people into hands qualified to attend them, even though he himself is frequently obliged to carry the sufferers to a mission or plantation hospital. Cavally Jones serves an area larger than the entire State of Connecticut and he can entertain you by the hour with stories which you might find hard to believe. He can demonstrate that a poultice made from termite mud and wrapped over a flesh ulcer or a filarial wound with a wilted banana leaf can be an effective remedy. He may even convince you of the merits of prescribing blindfolds to be worn at full moon by victims of a filarial worm that reputedly climbs up into the eyes during moonlit nights.

Deserving of mention and tribute are at least ten medical missionaries in rural Liberia whose work is as noble as that of David Livingstone. Among them is Nurse Jensen, a Norwegian-born and American-educated Lutheran missionary. Solely on her own resources and by her inexhaustible courage, Nurse Jensen has established a children's clinic in the jungle countryside of Santoya, some seventy miles beyond the road's end. For more than a quarter-century she has carried on her noble mission as the only white woman—indeed the only white person—in one of the most remote parts of all Africa. She regularly administers first aid and bedside care to the sick. She has repeatedly made smallpox, typhoid, and other vaccinations for an entire countryside. She puts quarantines into effect, sets broken bones, carries on extensive obstetrical practice, attends to ulcers, performs minor surgery, establishes sick camps, and during an uninterrupted succession of sixteen-to-eighteen-hour work days she maintains and directs the only children's clinic in her part of the world.

Although I consider Nurse Jensen one of the truly great women of this century, if I were asked to name the most heroic person in Liberian medicine today I should hesitate to answer. There are many heroes and heroines who might vie for that honor, including a great many devoted tribal medicine men and women and backcountry chiefs such as those of Gbanga and Saniquille in the central province, or Vonjamah-Kolahun in the western province. And other leaders of tribes or tribal villages continue to work valiantly to help their peoples and the Liberian Government in supplying at least a semblance of the medical and sanitation facilities that make the difference between life and death.

One may pay deserved tribute to the Liberian government for its strivings to meet the needs of public health administration. One can also praise the goals of the U. S. Public Health Service mission to Liberia, though not necessarily all of its specific administrative and working policies. Certainly one can praise the continuing work of Liberia's Department of Public Instruction in seeking to provide suitable courses in health and hygiene for the public schools.

But no folk medical arts can stop such international destroyers as malaria and filariasis or even the more localized diseases. The menace of the respiratory diseases, particularly of pneumonia and tuberculosis, keeps growing. Leprosy, though less common in Liberia than in Nigeria and much of French Africa, is also a serious problem. The venereal diseases, though not particularly virulent, require vigilance and painstaking countermeasures. Hookworm is widespread, calling for regular and determined control.

And again there is sleeping sickness. The tsetse fly carries the blood parasite that cause sleeping sickness in much the same way that anopheles mosquitoes carry the organisms that cause malaria. But only the female anopheles mosquito can carry the parasites of malaria. Both sexes of the tsetse fly propagate sleeping sickness; and the fly is a great deal hardier than any mosquito.

Firestone plantation surgeons have discovered that as many as one-third of the native tribespeople from certain inland areas show a positive reaction to gland punctures, the accredited test for identifying the presence of the organisms of sleeping sickness. Recently Dr. Karl Franz, a former Firestone surgeon stationed at Harbel, and Dr. David Weinman of the Harvard Schools of Medicine and Public Health, reported some early results obtained from treating African sleeping sickness with two arsenical preparations, both containing trivalent arsenic. One is Melarsen oxide; the other a drug called "70A" or phenylarsenoxide. The investigation was carried on in Liberia, under the auspices of the American Foundation for Tropical Medicine of New York, with the coöperation of the Firestone rubber plantations hospital at Harbel. Dr. Harold Rice, an outstanding authority on Liberian medicine, is a director of the Foundation.

In course of the Franz-Weinman experiment, twenty-six Liberians suffering from sleeping sickness — workers representing all the principal areas of Liberia — were treated with one or both of the drugs; sixteen were treated with Melarsen oxide alone; eight with 70A alone; and two with 70A followed by Melarsen oxide.

The latter drug was given orally to twelve patients, eight of whom showed neurological involvements that are common to the disease. After four months of treatment all the patients except one showed improvement, one case having

Typical Liberian countryside

A village in the interior

Raising the center pole for a native home

Thatching the roof

A native family

Making pottery

A forge

Liberian "country cloth"

Acrobatic dancers

Planting the seed of Hevea rubber

Sawing back seed-
ling rubber

Bud grafting on high
yielding strains

Tapping rubber

A rubber grove

Latex carriers bring in a morning crop

Preparing liquid latex for export

Processing

Drying

Baling for export

Tappers reporting for work

Firestone quarters for rubber workers

Planting cassava

A soccer game

Recess at a country school

A class in a Firestone school

Installation of thre native chiefs as pro vincial delegates i the Liberian Legis lature

President William V. S. Tubman makes his 1947 State of the Nation Address to the Legislature

relapsed. Four more patients, in earlier stages of the disease, were apparently cured by a single oral dosage of Melarsen oxide. The same drug was given intravenously to eight cases, three of whom were of the far advanced neurological types which had previously been treated unsuccessfully with other drugs. All patients in the early stages of the disease, and one in the advanced stage, reacted favorably.

Ten patients were treated with injections of the drug 70A, after preliminary tests of their sensitivity to it. Seven early-stage cases without neurological involvements became negative, having apparently been cured by one treatment of the compound, which is now considered highly effective in the initial stages of the disease. However, this newer drug is not particularly effective in the advanced stages, which usually show cerebral involvements, particularly depressive psychoses. These tend to lead into a condition of lethargy wherein the sufferer becomes too tired to eat or drink and presently unable to swallow.

The Franz-Weinman findings are supported by other research enterprises supervised by the American Foundation for Tropical Medicine. These include a prolonged clinical and field-station project carried on among the Liberian tribes under the direction of Dr. Everett P. Veach from 1941 to 1944.

Dr. Veach became interested in African sleeping sickness while serving as surgeon of a frontier hospital maintained at Cape Palmas by the Firestone Company. There the doctor's surgical assistant, a talented and well-educated Kru tribesman, contracted sleeping sickness and died. Dr. Veach began compiling clinical records of all sleeping-sickness cases brought to his attention and compared notes with government medical authorities of Liberia and the French Ivory Coast Colony.

In 1940 a chain of fourteen treatment centers for sleeping sickness was set up in tribe towns and villages by Dr. Veach, representing the Firestone Company; Dr. R. G. Fuszek, then director of Liberia's public health and sanitation department; and Dr. J. S. Seldon, surgeon for the Liberian Holy Cross Mission maintained by the Episcopal Church. The doctors began the program by teaching young natives how to use microscopes and to help with the necessary laboratory work.

Throughout a twenty-six-month period beginning early in 1943, between 200 and 400 tribespeople were examined each day and approximately 100 laboratory examinations were cleared daily: blood slides, gland punctures, spinal punctures, and microscopic examination of enlarged glands. Thousands of the sleeping-sickness sufferers traveled afoot from a hundred to two hundred miles along rough jungle trails to take advantage of the clinical services. Of 91,000 tribespeople examined, 13,481 (6,803 males and 6,678 females) were found to be suffering from sleeping sickness. About two-thirds of the sick people received more than six treatments, and the total of treatments reached 91,935 in Liberia alone.

About eight percent of all the patients treated were insane; about one-fourth had suffered from the disease for more than two years; and approximately half already suffered from drowsiness. Usually about two years of the infection leaves a condition of extreme drowsiness, accompanied by dull headaches. Presently lethargy sets in. As this progresses the sufferers frequently contract dysentery because of carelessness about food and drink, or pneumonia from sleeping on the damp earth or in the forests or jungle. If not, they presently reach a state wherein they are too tired to eat. Then others must feed them. In time they become too tired to swallow the food.

The depressive psychoses that characterize the progress of the disease usually make the patient passive and docile. Occasionally, however, the later-stage sufferer becomes violently insane when treated with drastic arsenic drugs. In the later stages of the disease the sick have vivid and sometimes terrifying hallucinations of lights and forest fires. They tell of hearing strange and terrifying noises. During the late stages the sufferers frequently run away from their homes and crawl or stagger to hide themselves in the dense bush, where they die of pneumonia or starvation or become prey to leopards or driver ants.

Trembling hands, trembling tongues, and enlarged knee joints are among other common symptoms of advanced cases. Flare-ups of fever are separated by long intervals of normal temperature. Deaths are most numerous among teen-age boys and girls, and next in the working ages from twenty to forty. Few babies or old people die of the disease. But the menace of sleeping sickness to youths and active adults is ever present. Medical authorities agree that continued research and aggressive operation of field clinics constitute the only possible defense against this ruthless disease.

The building and maintenance of hospitals is still another formidable medical problem for Liberia. As in most tropical countries, people rarely come to hospitals before or unless they are desperately sick. In all fourteen of the tropical countries where I have worked, a hospital is popularly regarded as a way point on the road to the cemetery. Particularly in rural Liberia, it is a sanctuary where one lies and struggles against the evil spirits, but from which one elects to go home to die.

Records of the Firestone hospital in the comparatively remote Cavally area near the French Ivory Coast show that the average confinement period for each patient is about twenty-six days—about twice the average confinement period in United States hospitals. The requirements for nursing care, medical administration, food, drugs, laundry, and other needs are proportionately great. And Liberia needs more hospitals desperately. The Liberian government has succeeded in maintaining a small public hospital at Monrovia and there are four mission hospitals, all small. Firestone remains the principal provider of hospitals.

And Liberia needs various other health facilities just as badly. Like the greater part of Equatorial Africa, she needs more water pipelines, chlorination plants, and sewer systems, along with facilities for purifying rural water supplies. Water-borne diseases are many, and their cure is primarily economic. Even Monrovia, the capital, has no dependable public waterworks, and the dry season usually finds well water being sold by the bottle or the gallon.

Money is the answer to another curse: hookworm. Hookworm is controllable, but control inevitably depends upon improved living standards — particularly a better diet and shoes for a predominantly barefoot nation.

As in other countries, the correlation between nutrition and disease is conspicuous, and this applies also to the problems of malaria control. Thanks to the use of antimalarial drugs that are now available, Liberia is making progress in her centuries-old fight against malaria. But much remains to be done.

The Negro's alleged immunity to malaria is a shabby fable. Negroes can and do have malaria; Liberians have suffered from it through the centuries, and they continue to suffer direly. Well-fed people have far greater resistance to this tropical devil than do the ill-nourished. When rice famines come, particularly when the tribes are forced to migrate from their homelands, malaria flares up. In Liberia as elsewhere a better agriculture is an effective defense against most diseases.

This generalization is as obvious as it is rudimentary. One soon realizes that the health of Liberia and the tribal agriculture of Liberia are one and the same. Diseased or disease-weakened people are virtually never good farmers; and, conversely, good farmers are not often sickly people. But good and healthy farmers, like any other vigorous people, can fall victim to epidemics and contagions. And the likelihood of such catastrophes is increased by the viciously circular nature of the general health problems: some forms of sleeping sickness destroy the work animals that would produce a more abundant agriculture and kill the cattle whose meat and milk would help to protect people from sickness.

When it comes to tuberculosis, the admission must be made that the situation is extremely discouraging. There are no statistical records of the incidence of tuberculosis in Liberia, but the grim facts are so apparent that statistical analysis is not necessary to establish the prevailing condition. Medical men and laymen alike know that the tuberculosis rate is formidable and that thousands of Liberians who escape such diseases as pneumonia, malaria, and sleeping sickness—which kill comparatively quickly—are marked for a somewhat slower death by TB. Tuberculosis, too, of course feeds on malnutrition and general poverty. But no single thing spreads it so fast as the native Liberian's hereditary fear of ventilation, of open doors or windows. The constant crowding of many persons into closed huts does to this disease very much the same thing that a strong, dry wind does to a forest fire. The only answer to this is widespread public education – the most difficult kind of education, the kind that is resisted most intensely.

Overall, the picture of health in Liberia has its brighter side, at least in terms of the future. Effective new insecticides such as DDT are reducing losses from malaria and similar diseases, though unfortunately there is as yet no such thing as a DDT or a sulfa drug for tuberculosis. There is crucial need for countless medical and public health measures in Liberia; but the way to improvement in most cases is known, and it is the means – in most cases money and trained personnel – that is lacking. The medicine man, despite the astonishing things he has been able to accomplish, is now an anachronism in view of the problems that confront the country. The answer is quite simple: Liberia can eventually conquer its worst disease problems, but it must have help to do so.

Chapter Eleven

Liberia Looks Ahead

THIS BOOK has suggested that Liberia is one of the most remarkable land areas in the world today and has sought to suggest some of the reasons why this is so. We have told of the birth and growth of the solitary African republic, its almost miraculous survival, its expanding resources, its stubborn integrity. We have tried to indicate that Liberia is a laboratory for democracy in one of the last great frontiers of the earth. We have pointed out, too, that Liberia is a strategic doorway into Africa for peoples of good will, and we have outlined some of her social and folk characteristics.

The United States has been tardy, perhaps understandably so, in appreciating the significance of the African nation which American Negroes helped to found. But our country is not alone in its tardiness. As recently as 1930 the Council of the League of Nations proposed officially that the Republic of Liberia be confined to a slender rim of the coastal front. That would have made it a mere federal district extending about forty miles inland and perhaps forty miles upcoast. The rest of the country – so the League proposal read – could best be mandated to a nation "expert in colonial administration."

The Liberian government protested strongly and eloquently. Edwin Barclay, President of Liberia during the bleakest of depression years, spoke for his country when he declared: "We shall never consent to those from the outside taking over control of the affairs of our government. If they do so it will have to be done by force." Through the tumultous years since 1930, as before, Liberia in one way or another has held its sovereignty.

The working Republic of Liberia does remain predominantly an institution of the coast, but its executive branch is directly responsible "for law and order, for life and limb, for weal or woe" of the peoples of the interior. Significantly Liberia is not a dictatorship and shows no symptoms of becoming one. The government's legislative branch, consisting of a senate whose members, like the President, are elected for six-year terms and a house of representatives with members elected for four-year terms, is alive and independent. The nation's constitution is bona fide. Citizenship remains limited to persons of African blood and elections are regular and orderly.

In current international affairs, Liberia participated in the United Nations Conference at San Francisco, and was or is a member of the United Nations Assembly, the United Nations Committee of Jurists at Washington, D. C., the International Aviation Conference at Chicago, the International Labor Conference at Paris, the Interim UNRRA Council at Montreal, the Monetary Conference at Bretton Woods, the United Nations Educational and Cultural Conference at London, and the Security Council.

In Monrovia, the opinions and beliefs of the jungle-filled interior mix with those of the world. French, British, American, and Liberian diplomats work, agree, and differ, as do the courts and the legislature. Backcountry chiefs call to present protests against the building of the new harbor at Monrovia on the grounds that the seaport will admit demoralizing influences. Other chiefs vehemently support the building of the great harbor. Chiefs from the far interior petition for more roads, schools, and clinics for their tribesmen. Other chiefs journey to the capital to point out the perils of windows, which produce lethal drafts. Others come to urge increased planting and storage of rice, more tribe schools, more adequate clinics for the too numerous sick in the tribes.

In the farthest backwoods common citizens ponder institutions and allegiances which only a few years ago were completely unknown. Recently, far down in the Cape Palmas country I met a tribesman who was undertaking self-instruction in law. At a mission school which he had attended for four months, Bolu had learned to read and write English. Currently he was sweating through several hard-used volumes of law texts. He confided eagerly: "I've just run across a book by a man named Blackstone. That book be plenty full with fine-fine thoughts."

Within five hours of Monrovia by jungle trail there lives a village chief with eighteen wives. They persuaded their husband to travel to the President's palaver and tell "government" that the great powers from far-off places were "making medicine" against Africa. En route the clan chief met an itinerant mission choir made up of native boys who walk the countryside and sing hymns in several native languages. The chief listened to the youths sing, heard their testimony regarding the good medicine of Christianity, and then invited them to follow him back to his village there to sing and explain their good medicine to his wives and other tribesmen. He did so on the highly logical grounds that it is better to make good medicine than to fear bad medicine.

Liberia now begins to grow together as a nation, and the coastal settlements founded by American Negroes and peopled by their descendants are at last beginning to blend into the less-known tribal interior. We have already noted how American Negroes have taken the lead in perpetuating the political structure of the Liberian republic. The list of Liberian presidents is one of common English and American names: King, Barclay, Thompson, Hubbard, and so on. But African names such as Twe, Fromoyan, Fo, Salaya, or Sobo have begun to appear on political rosters. They are still in the minority, but they are increasing. During November 1946 I attended the formal installation of three newly elected provincial representatives in the national legislature. The ceremonies took place in the Legislative Hall at Monrovia with house members, senators, cabinet members, diplomatic corps, the native soldiery, and citizenry as witnesses. All three of the provincials are paramount (tribal) chiefs from the interior; J. Boto Barclay, representing the Central province; Poo Derricks, the Eastern province; Flomo Fromoyan, the Western province.

President William V. S. Tubman, ex-officio chief of all Liberian chiefs, was present to administer the oaths of office. Dressed in the gold-and-black robe and crimson fez of a paramount chief, he moved with secure dignity, an attractive, medium-statured man, every inch an African, and honestly proud of it. He read the oaths to the succession of chiefs, who in turn raised their right hands and kissed the Bible. Then the President welcomed into the Liberian government the new chieftain-legislators from the far interior. He pointed out in scholarly but easily spoken English that on that day his country was entering a new era of maturity and unity. Later Chief Fo, speaking the Grebo language and interpreted by a youthful assistant or "messenger," proposed a toast to the "reborn democracy of Liberia." I believe that everyone looking on realized that we were beholding a rebirth of living democracy. The interior draws more closely to Monrovia as Liberia grows into autonomy.

Meanwhile Liberian life continues to mirror the old and the new, the changing and the changeless. In the rural spaces where roads have only recently appeared, the tribespeople are still not adjusted to the hell-for-leather travel habits of Americans, although American-built autos now weave along the increasing mileage of highways. About four hundred miles of new roads are under construction, including a through road from Monrovia across country to the French frontier.

Almost two-thirds of the land and somewhat more than two-thirds of the people of Liberia are beyond the reach of roads. Nevertheless, most Liberians are becoming increasingly aware of the outside world, particularly of the United States of America. The tribesman who has watched the shadows of big bombers sweep across his remote green valleys, who has seen by land the jeeps and the half-tracks of the U. S. Army, who has watched from afar the landing of troops or the building of a great harbor at Monrovia, has gained at least a fleeting glimpse of the great nation that can do so much for his own small one.

In the towns and in the countryside far beyond the towns, one can feel the warm sympathy of Liberians towards the United States, and observe the eager desire to accept the styles and fashions, the dance music and popular songs, the household furnishings, books and papers, bottled sodas and other gadgets of the mightiest of American nations. Tribespeople and American Liberians alike are eager to buy and use American goods, which to them are synonymous with a better life. Liberia is eager to learn about us, to know us better, to feel the warmth of our bona fide friendship. A generation ago, talented young men of Liberia studied in British and European universities and colleges. Particularly in England they acquired and brought home

British accents, modes of expression, styles in dress, and protocol. Today most young Liberians who are educated abroad are attending colleges, universities, and technical schools in the United States. They are taking home American attitudes and American enthusiasms.

But Liberia remains part of Africa, and it must help its youths to become educated as Liberians. Few other nations face public education problems as formidable as those of Liberia. For the past ninety years the country has labored and sacrificed to provide free public schooling for its people. Today the public school system carries on the struggle with extensive and welcome help from the mission schools in such outposts as Crozierville, Careysburg, Kakata, Sinta, Salala, and a dozen other frontier towns or villages.

Liberian statutes provide for the building and maintenance of public schools, secondary schools, and colleges, and for government-employed school supervisors. The law specifies minimum salaries for teachers. The planning and the beginning are conspicuously brave. But the achievement of adequate public education remains far away and almost indescribably difficult. General public school instruction goes no farther than the sixth grade, and high schools are exceedingly scarce. But the hope for founding a University of Liberia is still determinedly held by President Tubman and his administration.

Back in 1926 the American Advisory Committee on Education in Liberia, directed by James L. Sibley, completed a survey of public schools and mission schools throughout the republic. At that time American churches and other interested groups were contributing about a quarter-million dollars a year towards mission work in Liberia, the greater part of it in the field of education, though numerous appropriations for health, medical, and religious services were and still are deductible from the total. In 1926 the annual educational budget of the Liberian Government was $33,000. Of that amount $10,000 was for the support of Liberia College (at Monrovia), about $8,000 for the expenses of the republic's Department of Education, and approximately $15,000 for elementary schools for the entire country. At that time there were 56 elementary schools (principally one-room schools), enrolling 3,771 pupils and employing 63 teachers, all Liberians. During 1926 American and British church missions and other voluntary agencies were maintaining a total of 96 elementary or training schools staffed with a total of 235 teachers and providing places for 5,497 pupils. The work was noble, but the accomplishment was desperately inadequate.

By 1944 the Liberian Government was operating 78 schools enrolling 4,591 pupils and employing 160 teachers, with an overall education budget of $60,000, including $12,000 for the Liberia College at Monrovia and approximately $35,000 for the common schools. During the same year the number of mission and private schools had increased to 109, with enrollments totaling 7,131 and an estimated total of expenditures of $300,000 yearly. In 1944 the total budget of the Liberian Government was about one million dollars. Since 1944 the Liberian Government income has approximately doubled, and public school expenditures have more than doubled.

But the task is still formidable. The tribal youth of Liberia is particularly short of schools. The Secretary of Public Instruction and his assistants are recommending and working towards a number of highly laudable goals in public education. Included is a program of literacy for all people of Liberia (an undertaking similar to the mass literacy drives now current in Turkey and several colonies of

West Africa), which seeks to place at least one elementary school in every town or tribal community.

The Department of Public Instruction also seeks to establish more secondary schools in the interior – schools that can undertake the training of future teachers for elementary and tribe schools. The department proposes that more graduates of the projected public schools be admitted to the Booker Washington Institute for advanced training in agriculture and manual trades, and to the College of West Africa or to Liberia College for general studies. Meanwhile the Liberian government continues to grant scholarships to citizen students for advanced studies in the United States, or in West African schools such as Achimota College (the Gold Coast), Yaba College (at Lagos), or Fourah Bay College in Sierra Leone.

Any school system carries the responsibility of self-perpetuation. Schools help create the earning power that supports them, and they train and qualify the teachers who must presently keep and direct them. Liberia's need for native teachers is acute. One of the best sources is the Booker Washington Institute, one of the oldest American philanthropic interests in Liberia. The Institute was set up during the early 1920s as a manual training and general education center for Liberian youth, under the sponsorship of the American Advisory Committee on Education in Liberia. The Honorable C. D. B. King, at the time President of Liberia, called a conference of tribal chiefs who approved and dedicated the institution, to which the Government had contributed the building site and part of the initial money grant. By gradual and toilsome stages, the Booker Washington Institute has grown and developed. Products of the school's shops, including furniture, farm implements, and blacksmith products, are eagerly sought by the Liberian public. Booker Washington Institute graduates, the majority of whom are talented young tribe members, are in demand as farmers, craftsmen, teachers, and leaders of the people.

The Phelps Stokes Fund and the College of West Africa, the latter maintained principally by the Methodist Missionary Board, have increased the nation's educational resources, while President Tubman's administration has been seeking means to transform the College of Liberia at Monrovia into the University of Liberia, an undertaking as difficult as it is praiseworthy. In short, Liberia is doing its best, but is in crucial need of more schools, more citizen teachers, more schoolbooks, more school health services.

From the educational and medical points of view, another important event in Liberian history is now beginning to materialize — the establishment of an international institute for tropical medicine, with the active assistance of the Liberian government.

The idea of such a medical center is by no means new. Some forty years ago the Taft Commission recommended that the U. S. Government establish in Liberia a permanent institute for medical and other scientific research with particular reference to the study of tropical diseases, most of which are actually cosmopolitan diseases.

The Commission's recommendation was not acted on by the Congress, but private groups have worked toward the goal. There is, for example, the American Foundation for Tropical Medicine, administrative affiliate of the American Society and the American Academy of Tropical Medicine, which is the United States' only accredited organization in the field. Since 1940 the Foundation has been carrying on an extensive program of courses in tropical medicine, supporting research in the field, assisting important medical journals, and granting scholarships to selected medical students for advanced study.

Late in 1946 the President of Liberia, the American Foundation for Tropical Medicine, and Harvey S. Firestone, Jr., announced plans for founding the Liberia Institute, an international research center and clinic to be conducted under the sponsorship and direction of the American Foundation for Tropical Medicine. The Government of Liberia donated a suitable building site near the international airbase of Roberts Field, a short distance inland from the seaport of Marshall. As a memorial to Harvey S. Firestone and a centennial present to the Republic, the Firestone organization contributed the money to build and equip a hospital and a research laboratory.

In accepting the sponsorship of the Institute, the American Foundation for Tropical Medicine has agreed to maintain the research institute; to provide an annual operating fund of $115,000 for a period of five years; to enlist fourteen leading medical schools in the United States to supervise its direction; to select talented students who desire advanced training; and to maintain a continuing program for the study of the causes, effects, and treatments of tropical diseases. It is specifically stipulated that no restrictions of race, creed, or color will be applied to persons seeking training in the Institute, and that all knowledge secured from or through the Institute will be freely disseminated to all interested medical groups.

Among the medical school members of the American Foundation for Tropical Medicine participating in the direction of the Liberia Institute are the Harvard Medical School, Harvard University School of Public Health, Johns Hopkins University School of Medicine, Stanford University School of Medicine, Tulane University of Louisiana

School of Medicine, University of California Medical School, University of Southern California School of Medicine, University of Chicago School of Medicine, University of Michigan Medical School, Long Island College of Medicine, New York University College of Medicine, and Howard University Medical School.

The Liberian Government has insured the admission of qualified physicians regardless of their nationality. The American Foundation for Tropical Medicine has made plans and specific agreements for exchanges with several distinguished Old World schools, including the Liverpool, London, and Bombay schools of tropical medicine, the Pasteur Institute, and the refugee Hamburg Institute. Arrangements for exchange of research facilities have also been made with the Sierra Leone Field Station and numerous government and military medical services. Dr. Thomas W. Parran, Surgeon General of the U.S. Public Health Service, commented:

> "In my opinion, no single effort in this field is more worthy of wholehearted support. . . . When we consider the fact that just one tropical disease – malaria – constitutes the number-one health problem, we know there still is a big job to do in this sector. When we further realize that distant points no longer exist in the world – that this indeed is one world – we know also that it can be a world of disease or a world of health, depending upon how vigilantly we in medicine work for freedom from disease. . . . Our experience has shown a great need for study and control of tropical diseases on the West Coast of Africa. Teaching and research there will support greatly the efforts of the United States and subsequently the efforts of the World Health Organization. . . ."

The story of the Liberia Institute of the American Foundation for Tropical Medicine waits on time, talent, and work. It can place Liberia in the vanguard of research in world medicine, and further fulfill the Liberian conception of real education.

This concept of education is profoundly important to the Negro republic's place in the world. Education, by native definition, means the maintenance of public health; it means the understanding and use of the physical resources of Liberia – the immense forests, the fertile river valleys, the great iron deposits, the almost miraculous versatility of soils, and the many possible crops, of which natural rubber is a brilliant example.

The Liberian concept of education presumes the interaction of the emotions and the senses. It will not discard the old but will retain an appreciation of specific people and places, of changing seasons, of torrential rains and many-voiced drums, of the philosophic qualities of the tribesman who rests before his mud-and-thatch hut as motionless as a tree trunk, hands empty, his expression one of absolute peace.

Liberian education stresses the enduring value of the tribe, and of tribal democracy. It takes account of the fact that Liberia must forever remain one with Africa and must appreciate and utilize Africa's eternal resources.

During a single day of travel in Liberia one is likely to see such African extremes as the Negro Moslem who at sundown spreads his prayer rug and kneels facing Mecca; the tribal hut builder who blinks and coughs as he pats the mud walls of his new home and endures the smoke that cures the freshly laid thatch roof; the tribal smiths who shape jewelry of fine gold and alien silver and adorn it with the teeth and claws of leopards; the processions of head carriers; the tribesmen who weave and the tribesmen who spin; the itinerant country devil with robes dragging the ground, face hidden under a grotesque mask, head plastered with a formidable wig; the laughing drummer, the diligent scholar, the official in morning dress, the white-helmeted planter, the tribal poet, the long-robed trader, the sweating and almost naked farmer. All these are part of Liberia, part of the meaning and the significance of Liberia. Inevitably Liberian education must give self-knowledge to the people who make the nation real.

Such is the primer of Liberian education. Recently at Kakata I heard a stronger statement of it. The speaker was Saturday Fo, a twenty-year-old member of the Buzzie tribe who was shortly to enter the Booker Washington Institute at Kakata to study farming and carpentry. In this pursuit he hoped to be followed in turn by his three younger brothers, Forty, Friday, and Monday.

Saturday replaced his hat — a sort of miniature umbrella home-made of palm leaves and raffia fibers; he glanced downward at his broad bare feet, tightened the belt of his neat blue shorts, flicked a roving driver ant from his clean shirt front, and then turned to me. "Many moons go by and still Liberia live," he said. "Government be strong and proper. We go softly-softly. But we never lef' it. Liberia no finny."

This, then is the story of Liberia. It is a story of land and people, of resources and progress, of enterprise and expansion. It is a story of a nation founded by free men on the fringe of a great continent which thus far has had tragically little opportunity to learn what freedom means. The story of Liberia is without beginning and without end. For here the past and the present are but steps to the inspirational promise of the future.